AF473976

Some delights of the Rhône Valley

A Gastronomic Lyon
Glorious eating in France's capital of gastronomy (see p74)

B Majestic Hermitage
Scale the hill of Hermitage, one of the Rhône's most renowned vineyard sites (see p91)

C Within the walls of Avignon
Wander the cool, shaded streets of this magical city (see p109)

D Châteauneuf-du-Pape, the village and its wines
Walk up through the village to the ruined castle, then sample some of its legendary wines (see p60)

E The Dentelles de Montmirail
Visit the tranquil village of Gigondas nestled within the wild limestone massif of the Dentelles de Montmirail (see p64)

F The awesome Pont du Gard
A 2,000-year-old feat of engineering (see p91)

G The villages of the Luberon
A treasure trove of picturesque villages in a UNESCO Biosphere Reserve (see p93)

H Isle-sur-la-Sorgue Sunday market
Shop for local produce, homewares, clothes and antiques at one of the biggest and best open-air markets in Provence (see p87)

All prices are correct at time of going to press, but are subject to change.

Published 2025 by Académie du Vin Library Ltd
academieduvinlibrary.com
Founders: Steven Spurrier and Simon McMurtrie

Publisher: Hermione Ireland
Series editor: Adam Lechmere
Picture researcher: Silvia Lazzari
Design: Dan Prescott, Imago Create
Maps supplied by Cosmographics
Indexer and proofreader: Jenny Sykes
ISBN: 978-1-917084-68-0
Printed and bound in the EU
© 2025 Académie du Vin Library Ltd

All rights reserved. No part of this publication may be reproduced, stored in a retrieval system, distributed or transmitted in any form or by any means, including photocopying, recording or other electronic or mechanical methods, and including training for generative artificial intelligence (AI), without the prior written permission of the publisher. Translation into any other language, and subsequent distribution as above, is also expressly forbidden, without prior written permission of the author and publisher.

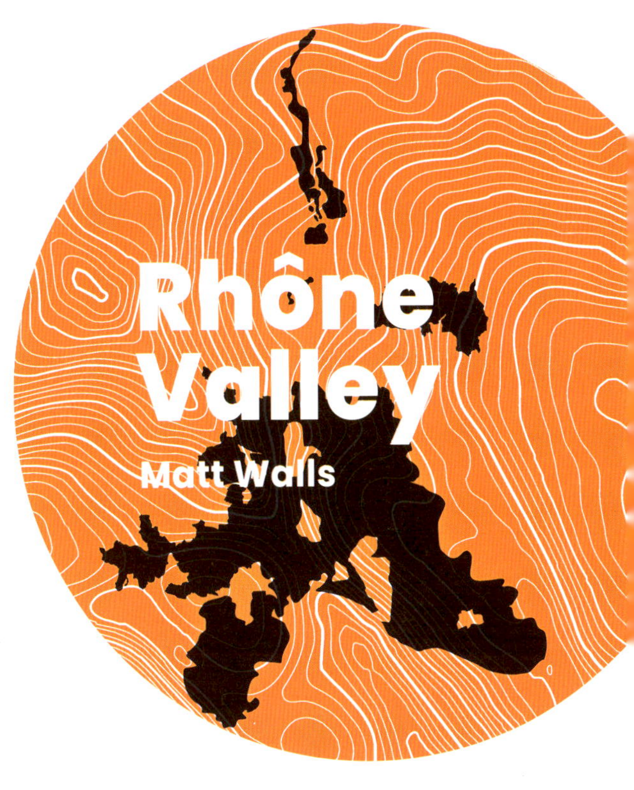

THE SMART TRAVELLER'S
WINE GUIDE

Contents

see p25

see p66

see p87

see p153

Bird's-eye view of Northern Rhône vineyards

Terraced vineyards of the Northern Rhône

Foreword

Wine has been made in the Rhône Valley for more than 2,000 years, at least since Greek settlers arrived from Anatolia in 600BCE, when they founded the city of Massalia – today's Marseille– and imported their viticultural skills. In the first century CE, the Roman author Pliny the Elder noted the popularity of the wines of Vienne, which were exported as far afield as Britain and Rome.

Later, when the Popes moved to Avignon, they planted extensive vineyards around the city – now the capital of Côtes du Rhône wines.

Over the centuries the region's renown grew; today, the wines of the Rhône Valley are universally prized, by collectors, wine aficionados and ordinary drinkers alike.

From the elegant reds of the Côte-Rôtie and Hermitage to the generous, sun-drenched blends of the southern Côtes du Rhône Villages, Luberon or Ventoux, there are few wine regions that can offer such diversity.

It is also important to remember that the Northern and Southern Rhône are very different. The south – olive groves, lavender plantations, fields of sunflowers and (of course) vineyards – is Mediterranean in character. The north is more rugged and dramatic, with terraces that follow the corrugated, vertiginously steep contours of the hillsides. These contrasting landscapes produce wines of a different style: northern reds tend to be fresh and juicy compared to the plumper, voluptuous reds and whites of the south.

But the Rhône Valley offers so much more than wine. With its tree-lined roads dappled with sunlight, its ancient villages, bustling squares, Roman theatres, medieval castles and quiet chapels, for many it's an archetypal vision of France.

Whether you're wine-curious, a collector with a cellar of the best Rhône wines, or simply a lover of southern France, this book will help you explore a region where every sip and every step brings you closer to the heart of French wine culture.

Philippe Pellaton
President of Inter Rhône

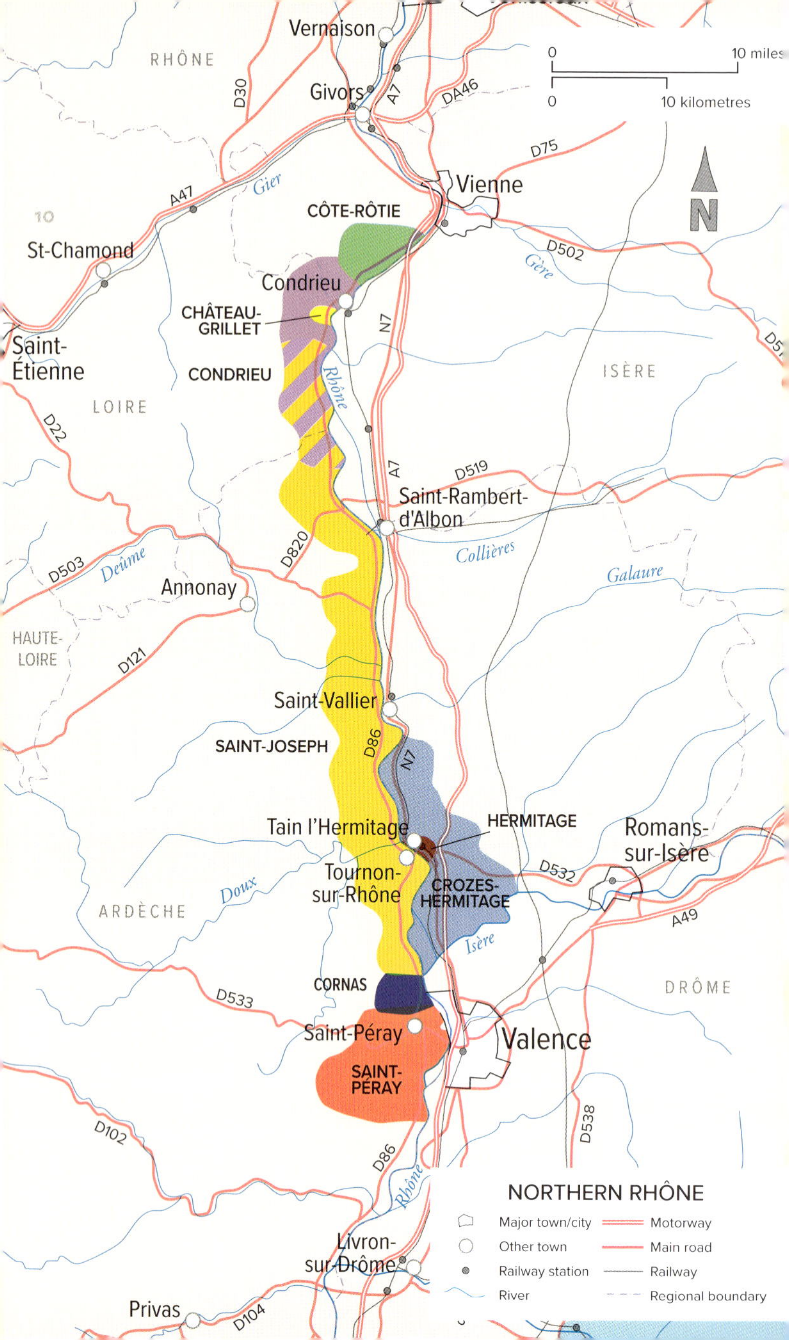
NORTHERN RHÔNE
0
10 miles
0
10 kilometres
N
Major town/city
Other town
Railway station
River
Motorway
Main road
Railway
Regional boundary
RHÔNE
LOIRE
HAUTE-LOIRE
ARDÈCHE
ISÈRE
DRÔME
10
Vernaison
Givors
Vienne
St-Chamond
Saint-Étienne
Condrieu
Annonay
Saint-Rambert-d'Albon
Saint-Vallier
Tain l'Hermitage
Tournon-sur-Rhône
Romans-sur-Isère
Saint-Péray
Valence
Livron-sur-Drôme
Privas
CÔTE-RÔTIE
CHÂTEAU-GRILLET
CONDRIEU
SAINT-JOSEPH
HERMITAGE
CROZES-HERMITAGE
CORNAS
SAINT-PÉRAY
Gier
Gère
Rhône
Collières
Galaure
Deûme
Doux
Isère
A7
A47
A49
DA46
D30
D75
D502
N7
D22
D519
D820
D503
D121
D86
D532
D533
D538
D102
D104

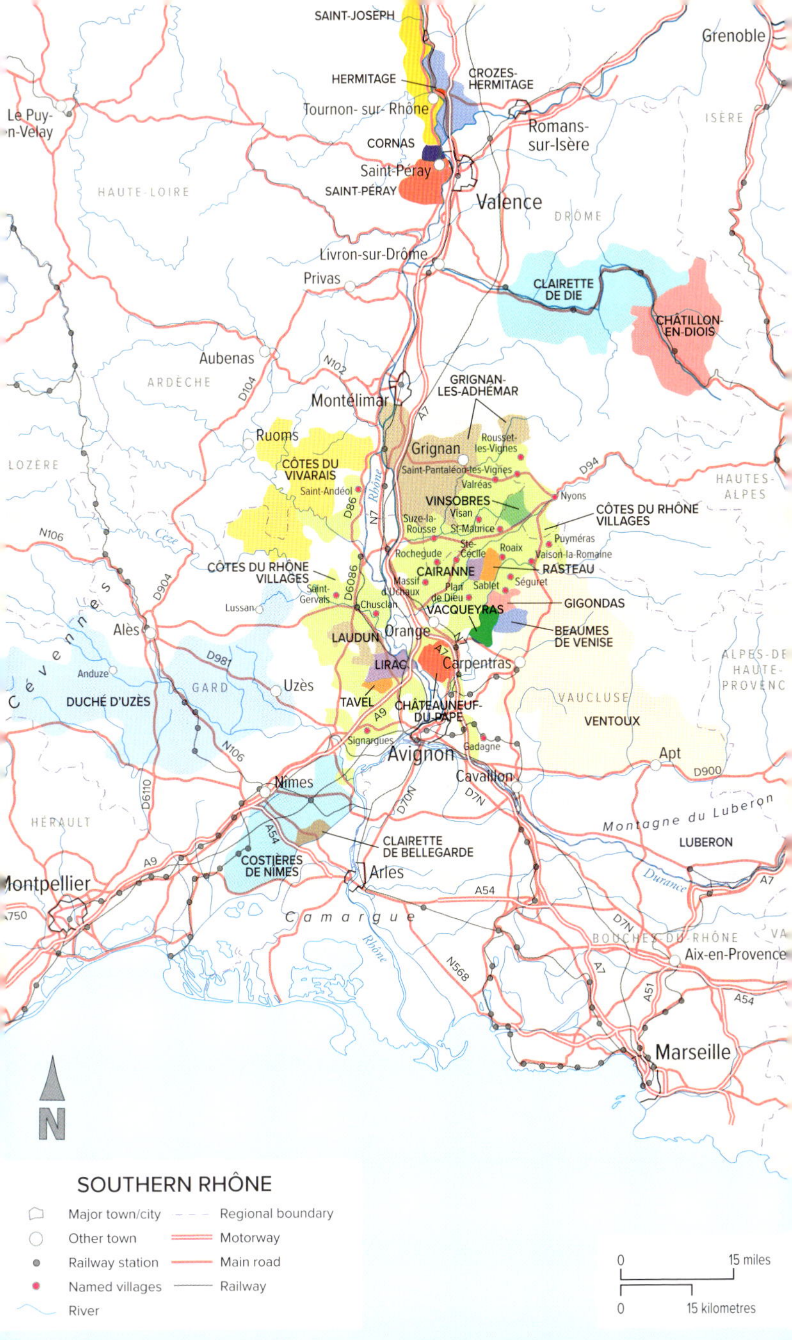
SAINT-JOSEPH
HERMITAGE
CROZES-HERMITAGE
Tournon-sur-Rhône
CORNAS
Saint-Péray
SAINT-PÉRAY
Valence
Grenoble
Romans-sur-Isère
ISÈRE
Le Puy-en-Velay
HAUTE-LOIRE
DRÔME
Livron-sur-Drôme
Privas
CLAIRETTE DE DIE
CHÂTILLON-EN-DIOIS
Aubenas
ARDÈCHE
N102
D104
Montélimar
A7
GRIGNAN-LES-ADHÉMAR
Rousset-les-Vignes
Grignan
Saint-Pantaléon-les-Vignes
Valréas
Ruoms
CÔTES DU VIVARAIS
Saint-Andéol
D86
Rhône
N7
LOZÈRE
D94
Nyons
HAUTES-ALPES
VINSOBRES
Visan
Suze-la-Rousse
St-Maurice
CÔTES DU RHÔNE VILLAGES
N106
Cèze
Rochegude
Ste-Cécile
Roaix
Puyméras
Vaison-la-Romaine
CAIRANNE
RASTEAU
CÔTES DU RHÔNE VILLAGES
Saint-Gervais
D6086
Massif d'Uchaux
Plan de Dieu
Sablet
Séguret
D904
Lussan
Chusclan
VACQUEYRAS
GIGONDAS
Cévennes
Alès
LAUDUN
Orange
BEAUMES DE VENISE
D981
Anduze
LIRAC
Carpentras
ALPES-DE-HAUTE-PROVENCE
GARD
Uzès
DUCHÉ D'UZÈS
TAVEL
CHÂTEAUNEUF-DU-PAPE
VAUCLUSE
VENTOUX
A9
Signargues
Gadagne
N106
Avignon
Apt
Cavaillon
D900
Nîmes
D6110
D70N
D7N
HÉRAULT
A54
CLAIRETTE DE BELLEGARDE
Montagne du Luberon
LUBERON
COSTIÈRES DE NÎMES
Arles
Durance
A7
Montpellier
A9
A54
A750
Camargue
D7N
BOUCHES-DU-RHÔNE
Rhône
N568
A7
Aix-en-Provence
A51
A54
Marseille
N
SOUTHERN RHÔNE
Major town/city
Other town
Railway station
Named villages
River
Regional boundary
Motorway
Main road
Railway
0
15 miles
0
15 kilometres

The Chapelle Saint-Christophe on the hill of Hermitage, overlooking Tain l'Hermitage and Tournon

Introduction

There is no better guide to a region than somebody who knows its wines. I've been visiting the Rhône Valley for two decades, and my search for its most delicious bottles has taken me to countless outposts that I would never have discovered otherwise – unspoilt villages in breathtaking countryside, with bustling markets among ancient houses and great places to stay and to eat.

Have you ever met a wine lover who isn't obsessed with food? Wine lovers always know the best places to eat, and if eating well is one of your priorities, the Rhône Valley is hard to beat. In the north, Lyon is France's capital of gastronomy. Further south, the wonderful climate and Provençal savoir-faire produce an abundance of local produce: olive oil, black truffles, cheese, charcuterie... not to mention the best sun-warmed tomatoes you'll ever eat.

When it comes to food and drink, this book doesn't just tell you the *what* and *where*, but the *who* – key wineries where you can meet and talk to local people who will really help you get under the skin of the place. After all, when you talk about wine, you can't help but touch on local history, geography, culture and traditions.

This is why I keep coming back to the Rhône – it's not just the food, the landscape and the climate, but the people. The wines here might be among the finest in the world, but they're often made simply by down-to-earth families that have been custodians of their land for generations. Winemakers here wear T-shirts, not suits.

So this book isn't just for wine geeks. It's for anyone looking to explore and appreciate this beautiful corner of France – whether you have two days, two weeks or two months. My aim has always been to help other people get the same enjoyment out of wine that I do – and by that, what I really mean is the same enjoyment out of life. This book will help you do that.

Matt Walls

History

The history of winemaking in southern France dates back to around 600 BCE. The domestication of the vine goes back considerably further elsewhere – in Iran and Georgia, for example, to around 5000 BCE. Nonetheless, it's fair to say the French have had more practice at making wine than most.

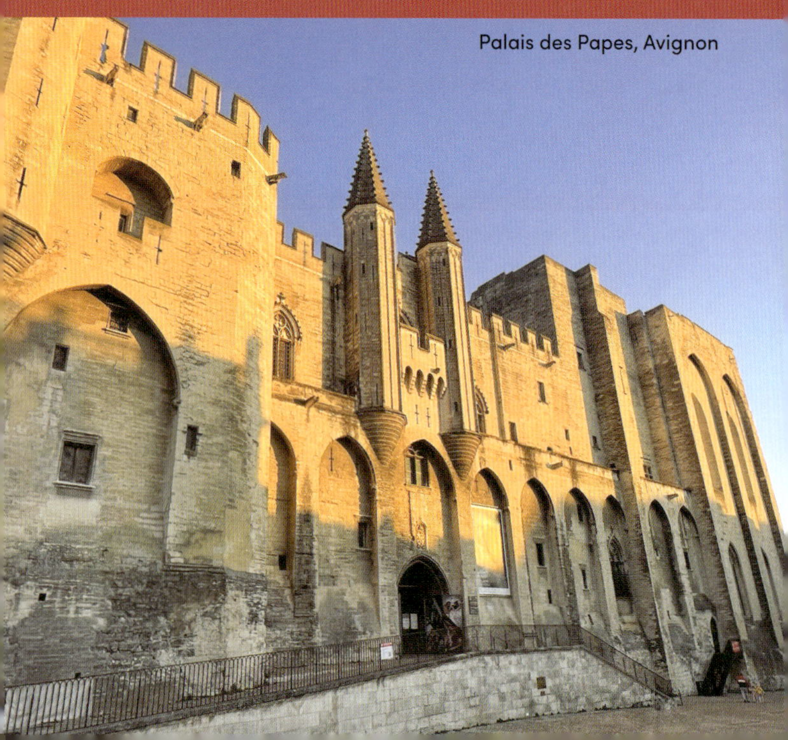
Palais des Papes, Avignon

Most of us drink wine primarily for the immediate pleasure it offers. But like most arts and crafts, to make sense of what's being made today – and why – it pays to know what has gone before. A sense of context and perspective deepens your drinking experience.

Rather than simply reading a book or admiring a painting, there's something about the act of consuming a bottle of wine that somehow plugs us into this long history; there's a sense of connection to an earlier time. The fundamentals of winegrowing haven't radically changed, so what we taste today isn't that far removed from what our ancestors would have tasted centuries ago.

So pour yourself a glass, and let's go back to the start. For the Rhône Valley, that means the ancient Greeks.

The Greeks and Romans (600 BCE – 476 CE)

Around 600 BCE, Greek settlers arrived in Southern France from Phocaea in Anatolia and founded the city of Massalia, known today as Marseille, close to where the Rhône river flows into the Mediterranean. One of the Greeks' many valuable imports was viticulture – they knew that vines grew happily alongside figs and olives, so they planted vineyards.

In the 2nd century BCE, Massalia came under Roman control, as it was an important stop on their trading route with Saguntum (present-day Sagunto, near Valencia in Spain). With the Romans, the vine spread further north. The Rhône has always been a vital communication route; fragments of clay amphorae used for wine storage have been found along the length of the river.

Greeks in Marseille

We know that vines have grown on the banks of the Rhône for over 2,000 years. Pliny the Elder (23-79 CE) tells us in his Natural History that in Vienne, near the vineyards of Côte-Rôtie, a local tribe called the Allobroges produced wines that were highly regarded and exported as far as Rome and Great Britain. Flavoured with resin, they would have tasted quite different to what we drink today.

The Western Roman Empire came to an end in 476 CE; local farmers no doubt continued to cultivate the vine, but documentary evidence becomes scarce until the Middle Ages, when the Church became a major player in the history of Rhône wines.

Papal parties (1309 – 1376)

From 1274 to 1791, a large enclave of southeastern France belonged to the Papal States, and in 1309 the seat of the papacy moved to one of the cities within its borders – Avignon, the informal capital of the Southern Rhône. This only lasted until 1376, but during that time seven popes took turns to live in the mighty Palais des Papes, which you can still visit today.

One of them, John XXII, built a summer palace in a village – since become known as Châteauneuf-du-Pape – 12km north of Avignon. The popes and their Roman household were a prodigiously thirsty bunch and their feasts were legendary. They quickly became enamoured with the local wines, and encouraged the planting of more vineyards to keep up with their needs. Even after they'd returned to Rome,

Pope John XXII

the papal court continued to receive shipments of their beloved Rhône wines.

In France, the opening of the Canal du Midi in 1681 helped Rhône winemakers transport their wares throughout France and beyond. By the 17th century, Rhône wines had built a name for themselves and were held in increasingly high esteem – so much so that when Louis XIV presented Charles II of England with 200 barrels of fine wine, he included some Hermitage among the Champagne and Burgundy.

Vineyard armageddon (1862 – 1868)

The fortunes of the Rhône went from strength to strength, with the wines of the west bank of the Southern Rhône gaining particular favour from the 1600s. But all of this came crashing down with the accidental import of phylloxera, a ravenous aphid that attacked the roots of the vine and that went on to almost completely destroy the vineyards of France.

Phylloxera arrived in 1862 in Lirac, to the north of Avignon, in a shipment of vines from Mr Carle in the USA to his friend M. Borty, who planted them in his garden. From there a plague of these bugs spread to neighbouring villages, killing vines as it went by attacking their roots. American vines were naturally impervious; French vines were not – and it took until 1868 for experts to figure out what was causing their vines to die. It was even longer until a cure was found – grafting French vines onto American rootstock. By this time, it had destroyed 2.5m hectares of French vineyards.

The birth of appellations (1923 – 1936)

Some vineyards were never replanted, others only gradually. The most famous vineyards, such as those of Châteauneuf-du-Pape, were making wine again by the mid-1880s: the Pope's stamp of approval served local winemakers well, and there was demand throughout Europe and beyond. Unscrupulous winemakers from other regions took advantage of its renown, however, branding their own (often inferior) wines as Châteauneuf-du-Pape in order to charge higher prices.

It came down to Baron Le Roy de Boiseaumarié (1890–1967), the owner of Château Fortia in Châteauneuf-du-Pape, to do something about this fraudulent behaviour. He was a lawyer, and neighbouring winemakers implored him to stamp it out. He eventually agreed, and in 1923 set out an official growing area, deciding which grape varieties were permitted, and proposing rules of production which made for a genuine Châteauneuf-du-Pape. After 10 years, he was successful, and by 1936 his home village was the first official wine appellation in France (well, by one day; four other appellations – Arbois, Cassis, Monbazillac and Tavel – were granted the following day). His method laid the framework for the *appellation d'origine protégée* (AOP) system for wine appellations across France, and now throughout Europe.

Pierre Le Roy de Boiseaumarié

The World Wars and their aftermath 1945–56

World Wars I and II devastated France, its people, the French wine industry and its wine culture. Many winemakers had been killed; vineyards that were difficult to cultivate – those that were steep and inaccessible, for example – were abandoned, though it's often these hillside sites that give the best wines. After World War II, few people in France could afford fine wine – quantity was more important than quality. It took time for France to rebuild.

In February 1956, there was another event that changed the Rhône landscape forever. It was the coldest month in France since 1900, when records began. Temperatures dropped to minus 20°C, and a freezing north wind reached speeds of 180kmh. Just beforehand, it had been unseasonably warm, and the sap in the olive trees had started to rise; the sound of screaming was heard from the trees as the sap froze, splitting their trunks. The olive groves of the Southern Rhône were decimated.

Since olive trees take so long to grow and bear fruit, instead of replanting with saplings, farmers planted vines, as they give a crop within three years. Until this point in the Rhône, family farms were largely polycultural, growing multiple different crops; 1956 marks the change towards a more monocultural way of working.

Going green (1978 – present day)

After World War II, the winegrower's work became easier thanks to easier access to heavy machinery and the spread of agrochemicals. These insecticides and herbicides were widely adopted during these hardscrabble years, as they meant winemakers could ensure larger and more reliable crops.

By the end of the 1970s, a growing contingent of winemakers had turned their backs on synthetic chemicals, in a search for a more sustainable and environmentally sensitive way of working. This became more widespread in the 2000s, and by the 2023 harvest, 20% of the vineyard area producing AOP wines in the Rhône Valley was certified organic.

Today, the finest wines of the Rhône Valley are considered the equals of those from Bordeaux and Burgundy, and fetch hundreds – if not thousands – of pounds per bottle. They're sought by wine collectors from New York to Hong Kong, and fans of Rhône wines are famously fanatical about this captivating, soulful region.

Hospitality in a bottle

The Rhône Valley is one of France's most storied and seductive wine regions – a land where centuries of viticultural tradition meet the warm pulse of the Mediterranean.

For the wine enthusiast eager to pair exceptional tasting experiences with cultural richness and stunning landscapes, the Rhône Valley offers a journey as memorable as the wines themselves.

Stretching from the ancient city of Vienne down to the sun-soaked environs of Avignon, this region – France's second largest vineyard for AOC wines – is a mosaic of vineyards, hilltop villages and passionate winemakers, all waiting to be discovered by the smart traveller.

What sets the Rhône apart is the astonishing diversity and quality of its appellations. From the spicy reds of northern Crus like Saint-Joseph and Cornas, to the generous southern whites such as Lirac and Vacqueyras, not forgetting the delicious sparkling Clairette de Die, each glass tells the story of its terroir.

The region champions both powerful and nuanced styles, with reds, whites and rosés that can delight every palate. From the intensity of Syrah to the floral lift of Viognier, the Rhône offers a spectrum of wines crafted with skill and integrity.

But this is not just a destination for tasting – this is a place to experience wine. The Rhône Valley invites you to slow down and immerse yourself. Wander through stone-built villages bustling with weekly markets; share rustic, sunlit meals with winemakers; explore Roman theatres, medieval castles and art-filled chapels nestled among the vines.

Whether you're drawn to lively harvest festivals, curated wine routes or tranquil countryside stays, the region's oenotourism offers something for every curiosity and mood. For the gourmet, the Rhône is a feast. Truffle-laced dishes, seasonal vegetables and creamy goat's cheeses reflect the land's generosity, perfectly matched by local wines.

Those with an eye for beauty will be charmed by the pastel-toned vineyards in autumn or the lavender-scented roads of summer. History lovers can follow routes from antiquity to the Renaissance, while culture seekers can revel in music festivals and artisan workshops. The Rhône Valley doesn't just produce great wines – it welcomes you into a way of life where wine, food, history and hospitality are seamlessly intertwined.

Content supported by Rhône Valley Vineyards

Geography

Leaving aside the wealth of food and wine in the Rhône, the valley is also one of the world's most beautiful landscapes. When considering its geography, remember that its famous countryside – not to mention its climate – is very different from north to south.

The vineyards of Hermitage

North and South

They share a river and some grape varieties, but aside from that, the Northern and Southern Rhône are very different.

The Southern Rhône is by far the larger of the two regions, producing over 90% of the wine of the entire Rhône Valley (in wine terms 'the Rhône Valley' refers to the Northern Rhône plus the Southern Rhône and satellite appellations). It is a vast basin, from the foothills of the Cevennes mountains in the west to Mont Ventoux in the east; from the Camargue wetlands near the Mediterranean up to the town of Montélimar. Its capital is Avignon, a vibrant and colourful city, and there are countless other ancient towns and pretty villages to visit through the area. Though it's hard to generalize due to the size of the region, the landscape here is largely Provençal, with olive groves, lavender plantations, fields of sunflowers and – of course – endless rows of vines. There are hills and mountainous areas on the fringes, but much of the terrain here is fairly flat.

The Northern Rhône is very different. While the vineyards of the Southern Rhône stretch further west to east than they do north to south, the opposite is true in the north – the vineyards here stick tightly to the banks of the

Vienne

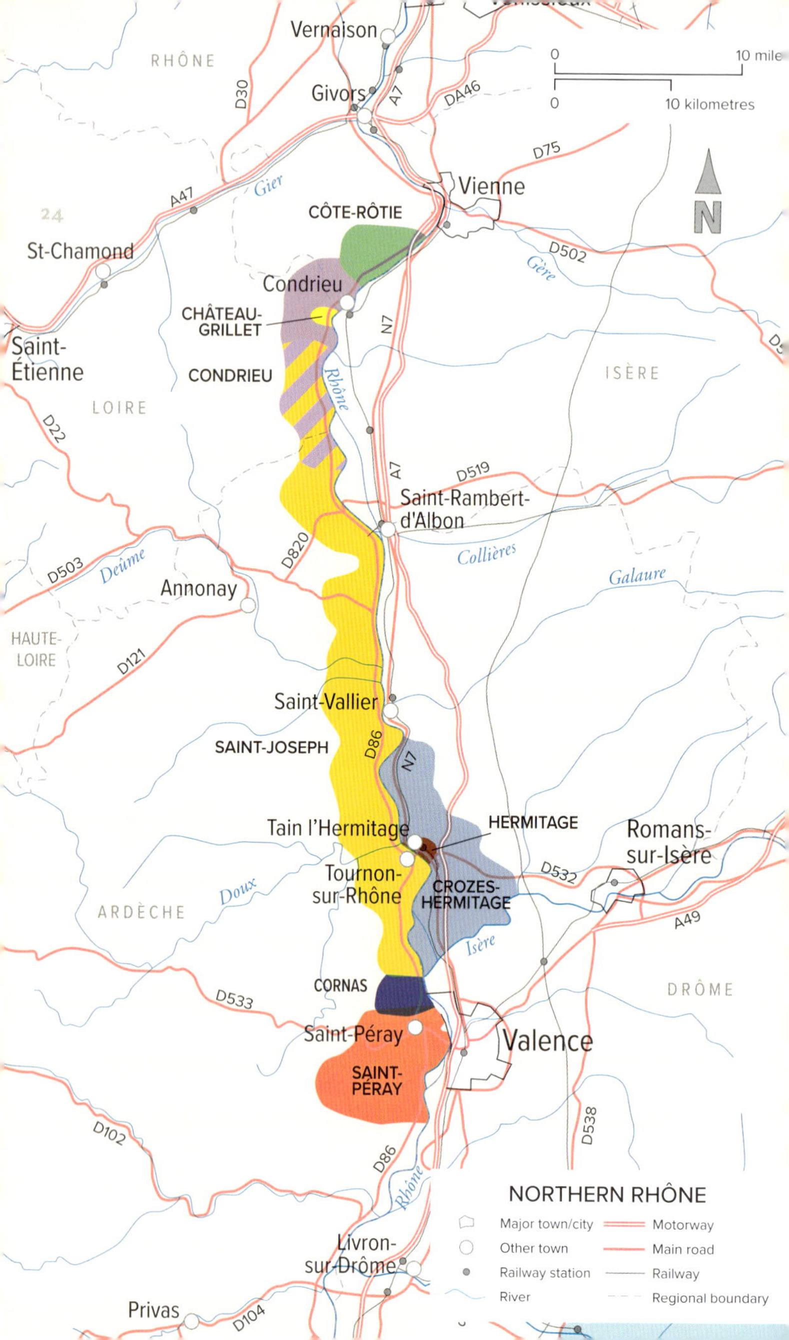
Vernaison
RHÔNE
D30
Givors
A7
DA46
0
10 miles
0
10 kilometres
D75
Gier
Vienne
A47
24
CÔTE-RÔTIE
N
St-Chamond
D502
Gère
Condrieu
CHÂTEAU-
GRILLET
N7
Saint-
Étienne
CONDRIEU
Rhône
ISÈRE
LOIRE
D22
A7
D519
Saint-Rambert-
d'Albon
Collières
D820
D503
Deûme
Galaure
Annonay
HAUTE-
LOIRE
D121
Saint-Vallier
SAINT-JOSEPH
D86
N7
Tain l'Hermitage
HERMITAGE
Romans-
sur-Isère
Tournon-
sur-Rhône
D532
CROZES-
HERMITAGE
Doux
ARDÈCHE
Isère
A49
CORNAS
DRÔME
D533
Saint-Péray
Valence
SAINT-
PÉRAY
D102
D538
D86
Rhône
NORTHERN RHÔNE
Major town/city
Motorway
Other town
Main road
Railway station
Railway
River
Regional boundary
Livron-
sur-Drôme
Privas
D104

Rhône river as it runs from Vienne in the north (just south of Lyon) to the town of Valence. The landscape here is more dramatic, with row upon row of slim terraces that follow the corrugated contours of the hillsides, some of which are vertiginously steep. You can't help but feel for the poor growers, having to scale these slippery slopes in the baking heat. The upkeep of the dry stone walls is a job in itself. Getting tractors up these hillsides is impossible; everything has to be done by hand. When you see what viticulture entails in the Northern Rhône, it makes every drop that much more precious.

It's a greener landscape than the Southern Rhône, more wooded and wild, and while it doesn't have the honey-coloured sandstone villages of the south, for food and wine lovers, several of the towns here are well worth visiting. Lyon for one is a global mecca for gourmets, and while it's strictly speaking outside of the Rhône Valley, we are including a few of its attractions (see p83), as it's a great place to start your Rhône journey.

Soils – why they matter

Why are the two parts of the Rhône Valley so distinct? It's all down to geology. The Rhône emerges from the Rhône Glacier in the canton of Valais in the Swiss Alps, and it flows

Châteauneuf-du-Pape *galets roulés* or 'pudding stone' soils

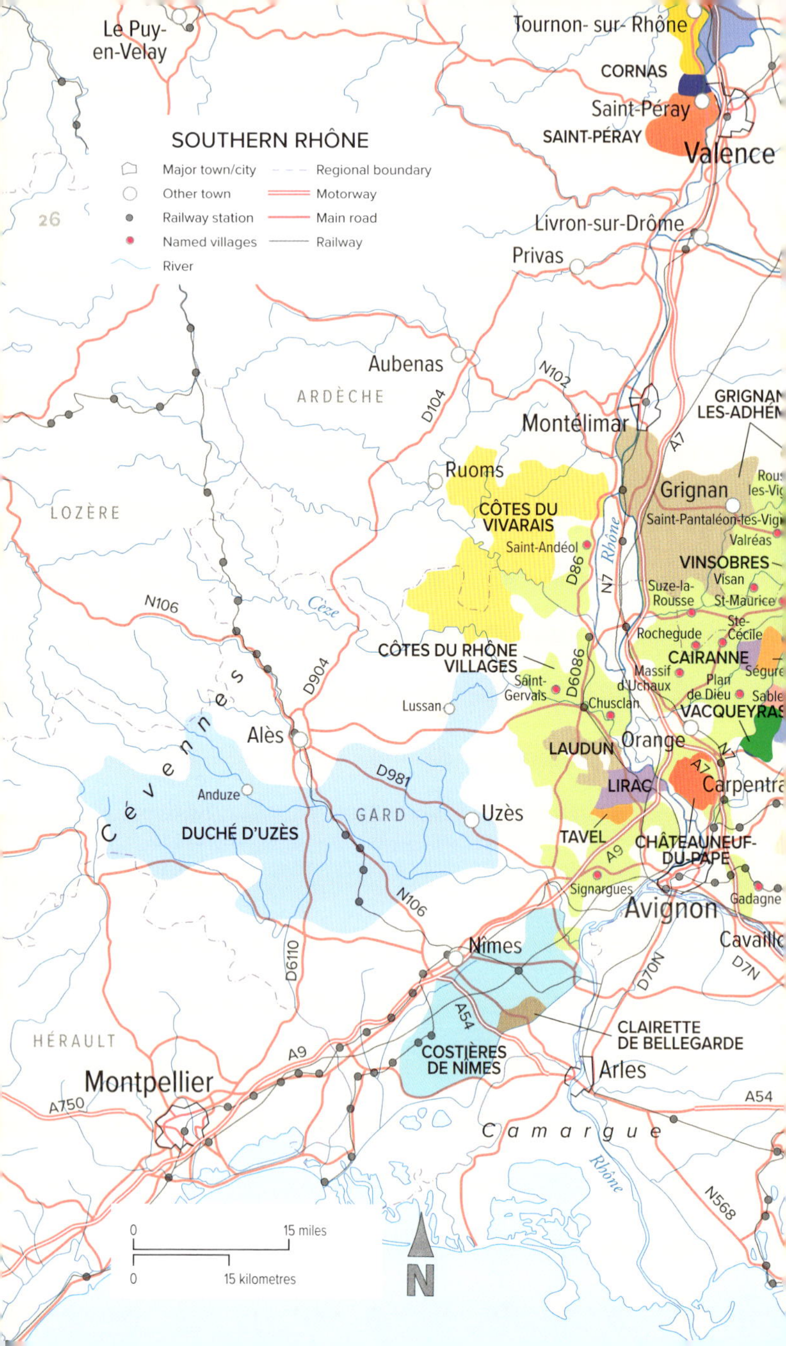
SOUTHERN RHÔNE
Major town/city
Other town
Railway station
Named villages
River
Regional boundary
Motorway
Main road
Railway
Le Puy-en-Velay
Tournon-sur-Rhône
CORNAS
Saint-Péray
SAINT-PÉRAY
Valence
Livron-sur-Drôme
Privas
Aubenas
ARDÈCHE
N102
D104
Montélimar
GRIGNAN-LES-ADHÉM
A7
Ruoms
CÔTES DU VIVARAIS
Saint-Andéol
Grignan
Saint-Pantaléon-les-Vig
Valréas
VINSOBRES
Visan
St-Maurice
Suze-la-Rousse
Rochegude
Ste-Cécile
CAIRANNE
Ségure
Massif d'Uchaux
Plan de Dieu
Sable
VACQUEYRAS
LOZÈRE
N106
Cèze
D86
N7
Rhône
D6086
D904
CÔTES DU RHÔNE VILLAGES
Saint-Gervais
Chusclan
Lussan
Cévennes
Alès
Orange
LAUDUN
LIRAC
Carpentra
D981
Anduze
DUCHÉ D'UZÈS
GARD
Uzès
TAVEL
A9
CHÂTEAUNEUF-DU-PAPE
Signargues
Avignon
Gadagne
Cavaill
N106
D6110
Nîmes
D70N
D7N
A54
CLAIRETTE DE BELLEGARDE
HÉRAULT
COSTIÈRES DE NÎMES
Arles
Montpellier
A750
A9
A54
Camargue
Rhône
N568
0
15 miles
0
15 kilometres
N

west, via Geneva, into France, through Lyon – then drifts more or less due south towards Valence.

This stretch is referred to as the Northern Rhône, and the soils are fairly uniform. The reason the river flows so fast and deep here is that it hits the edge of the Massif Central, a huge slab of 300-million-year-old granite that underpins much of central and southern France. The river's course is dictated by this bedrock, which directs it south, towards the Southern Rhône.

At the southern tip of the Northern Rhône, the granite is replaced with more sedimentary soils: limestone, sandstone, clay and pebbles. These are more easily influenced by the flow of the river, so from here it snakes around, changing its course over millions of years, and creating tributaries as it reaches Avignon. Here, it dog-legs to the west and heads off to the Camargue and eventually the Mediterranean. As it goes, it lays down multiple banks of large, rounded alluvial stones, known in the Rhône as *galets roulés* – the famous 'pudding stones' of Châteauneuf-du-Pape.

Avignon

So geology explains why the region looks as it does. But its importance doesn't end there; different types of rock and soil can have an influence on the wine, so expect to hear winemakers talk a lot about the different soils they have in their vineyards. Vines grown on clay tend to give wines with richness and voluptuous textures; those grown on sand tend to express finesse rather than power; limestone can produce a feeling of freshness and energy that is particularly welcome in white wine; and granite often gives wines an upright, saline nature.

Bless the weather, curse the storm

Soil is just one influence on wine. Another is topography: vineyards at high altitude tend to be cooler; whether they are flat or sloping can have an effect on ripening and water supply; and the direction they face is important too – in the northern hemisphere, south-facing means plentiful sun, while north-facing suggests a cooler, shady site.

Another major influence is climate. The Southern Rhône is reliably hot in summer; even in April the weather tends to be warm and sunny. It's also quite dry here, again particularly in summer – the rains usually come in autumn and winter. This glorious weather is one of the reasons why it's so popular with tourists, with temperatures regularly over 30°C (occasionally topping 40°C) in July and August.

Though the Northern Rhône is still warm and sunny in spring and summer, it's noticeably cooler and rainier. The climates are distinct enough for these two regions to grow different grapes: many varieties they grow in the south wouldn't fully ripen in the north (see Styles and grapes p32)

What both ends of the Rhône Valley share is a blustery north wind; in the Southern Rhône it's called Le Mistral, in the Northern Rhône they call it La Bise. Either way, when it blows you'll know about it – it's strong enough to overturn chairs and tables on café terraces. Locals say that it blows on average one day in three, but the reality is that it's less common that this; they also say it never blows for an even number of days – so it will visit for one, three or five days in a row. It can make working the vineyards here particularly challenging, but winemakers consider it a natural antiseptic, drying the vineyards after rain and banishing fungal diseases.

'Rainfall patterns have changed – instead of showers all year round, winemakers are seeing heavy storms in autumn and winter, then drought in summer'

The grapevine is a sensitive plant. Through the flavour of its wine, it can express incredibly subtle differences in terroir – that magical, untranslatable word which encompasses everything that can affect the vine (or anything that grows): soil, topography, climate, grape variety – and human influence as well.

The vines have certainly noticed the change in climate in the Rhône since the 1970s. The most obvious, measurable change is that picking dates are on average a couple of weeks earlier. Rainfall patterns have changed too: instead of rain showers falling all year round, winemakers increasingly observe heavy storms in autumn and winter, then drought conditions during the summer.

But winemakers aren't sitting still. Some are planting newly authorized grape varieties that are well adapted to drought conditions, such as Carignan Blanc. Others are innovating with new techniques, such as spraying wet clay onto the vines, which acts like a natural sunscreen.

If the climate continues to change at the same pace, no doubt we'll see vineyards gradually climb the slopes of Mont Ventoux in search of cooler and wetter weather. Or perhaps we'll see a resurgence of the Port-style sweet reds of Rasteau. Either way, it's an unsettling time to be a winemaker – not just here, but everywhere.

Mont Ventoux

The Théâtre Antique de Vienne

Styles and grapes

The Southern Rhône is a huge region with multiple microclimates. So the reds here range from medium-bodied and ruby-coloured with crisp berry fruits in the cooler mountain fringes – all the way to thunderous, booming, powerful wines in the hottest, driest areas.

Chapelle Saint-Christophe, Hermitage

The fresher Northern Rhône produces red wines with a tighter stylistic range. They're typically medium-bodied, with more refreshing acidity and a slightly drier texture – they're not as fluid and plump as the wines of the south, and are more floral and spicy.

This isn't down to climate alone – it's also down to the grapes they grow. Northern Rhône reds get their aromatic side from Syrah – it's the only red grape cultivated here, and that's the style of wine it gives. In the Southern Rhône, almost all reds are blends of different grape varieties, but majoring on Grenache, which produces a richer, more strawberry-flavoured wine.

The whites follow the same pattern – from fresh and juicy to voluptuous in the Southern Rhône, and more medium-bodied in the North. Both can be delicious but the Northern Rhône is more consistent in style and quality.

Rosé is only made in the Southern Rhône – there's no tradition of pink wines in the north. There are two contrasting styles. Firstly, the ubiquitous pale, dry style that's become world famous thanks to Provence (which is, after all, right next door to the Rhône). They don't demand much thought and are crisp and refreshing on a hot day. The other style is the 'traditional', darker-coloured rosé. The Southern Rhône was once famous for this style (in the Cru of Tavel, specifically), and – though unfashionably dark in colour – they can have real depth, complexity and food-friendliness. Some can even age for decades – rare for a rosé.

All of the above comments relate to dry wines. Wines are either fully dry or very sweet in the Rhône; there's nothing in between. There aren't many sweet wines, but they can be a delicious treat. In the Southern Rhône, Muscat de Beaumes de Venise has been made for over 2,000 years, and sweet Rasteau (called Rasteau Vin Doux Naturel, meaning Natural Sweet Wine), is reminiscent of young Port. In the Northern Rhône, sweet wines are rarer still.

Sparkling wine is more common in cooler climates, so you won't find much here – except in the little Northern Rhône Cru of Saint-Péray.

Who makes your wine?

In the Rhône, winemakers are split into three main families: private wine estates, cooperative wineries and merchants known as *négociants*.

There are around 1,600 private estates in the Rhône Valley. Often with names that begin with *Domaine* or *Château*, they range in size from just a few hectares to 100 hectares or more.

There are also around 90 cooperative wineries in the Rhône Valley. These winemaking facilities, all but a few of which are in the Southern Rhône, are owned by grower collectives. Some co-ops might comprise just a dozen or so families pooling their resources; other co-ops are titanic structures pumping out millions of bottles a year. They tend to be very good at value wines, but rarely make the best wines in the valley. Excellent examples include Les Vignerons d'Estézargues, Maison Sinnae and La Cave de Cairanne.

The largest amount of wine from the Rhône Valley is produced by merchants known as *négociants*, of which there are over 400 working in Rhône. Rather than owning all their own vineyards, négociants buy grapes, grape juice or finished wine, then bottle it and sell it under their own brand. Some are stronger than others, but the best have some exceptional wines in their (often extensive) ranges. Leading négociants include Guigal, Chapoutier and Delas.

Northern Rhône grapes

The Northern Rhône is smaller and easier to get your head around than the Southern Rhône. One reason for that is the limited number of grapes they work with – all of which have migrated to the Southern Rhône too, where they give slightly different expressions.

Winemaking trends: stems

Adding stems to the fermentation vats for red wines is a practice that goes in and out of fashion. Including the stalks doesn't sound very appealing; after all, you wouldn't want to eat one. But in a warming climate, stems bring certain advantages. They add some herbal nuances to the flavour of the wine, bringing complexity and freshness; they add texture to the wine; they slightly reduce the alcohol content by soaking it up. But they have disadvantages too: they can reduce the overall acidity, and they can make a wine taste tough or rustic, especially when it's young. Before the destemming machine was widely adopted, no wines were destemmed. And using stems is a trend that's catching on again. M. Chapoutier, for example, used to destem all their reds, but are now incorporating a proportion into their top wines. Others, such as the excellent Domaine Marc Sorrel in Hermitage, use all the stems they can.

Syrah

Syrah

The only red grape grown in the Northern Rhône. One of Syrah's synonyms is Shiraz, which happens to be the name of a city in Iran. This has led some to wonder whether this variety has Persian roots – but DNA analysis has shown that it originates in the Northern Rhône. It produces wines with freshness and crunch here, inky-purple in colour, with flavours that range from blackberry and raspberry to black olives, black pepper, crispy bacon and violets. The lighter-bodied styles are made in Crozes-Hermitage and Saint-Joseph; Cornas and Hermitage are more concentrated and tannic. Côte-Rôtie is particularly fragrant, and stylistically between the two. In the Southern Rhône it's the second-most-planted grape behind Grenache, where the hotter climate and richer soils make for a more muscular, potent style of Syrah.

Viognier

Viognier

Another grape that originates from the northerly tip of the Northern Rhône, Viognier is highly distinctive. It might be relatively cool here, but the grape produces luxurious, satin-textured whites that glide across your tongue, with heady aromas of peach, apricot and jasmine. It might be grown all over the world now, but Condrieu remains the finest expression. In the Southern Rhône, it's more voluptuous still, and is usually used to add a certain richness and a floral flourish to white blends.

Marsanne

Marsanne

In the southern half of the Northern Rhône, for white wines they grow exclusively Marsanne and Roussanne, which are usually blended together. Marsanne is more common as it's easier to grow, giving quite assertive wines with complex aromatic palettes: honeysuckle, apricot, peach, mango, rhubarb... then honey and toasted nuts as they age – Marsanne from Hermitage can last for decades.

Roussanne

Roussanne

Northern Rhône Roussanne is similar in weight to Marsanne, and aromatically it has more white-fleshed allusions: pear, lychee, white flowers. While Marsanne is only rarely found in the Southern Rhône, Roussanne is very common – and it gives a much richer, more powerful style of white in this warmer climate, that's often aged in oak barrels to produce flamboyantly delicious wines.

Winemaking trends: oak

Using oak barrels to mature wines has a long tradition on the Rhône Valley, particularly in the Northern Rhône. The contents undergo a very gradual oxygenation through the staves, which softens harsh tannin and creates a more elegant texture. If the barrels are new, they also contribute flavour – sweet spices, cola, clove, tobacco, coconut and vanilla are all flavours that might be derived from new (or fairly new) barrels. This was fashionable in the 1990s and 2000s, but today the trend is to use less new oak, with many winemakers favouring old barrels or containers made of other materials such as concrete or clay. Guigal is famous for maturing its top Côte-Rôties for years in new oak barrels; Domaine du Coulet in Cornas makes excellent Cornas without any wood in sight.

Southern Rhône red grapes

While the Northern Rhône only uses one grape for its reds, the Southern Rhône has over a dozen to choose from – a cornucopia of different varieties they can choose from and blend together. Some are much more common than others, however, and the most ubiquitous is Grenache.

Grenache

It's surprising how central Grenache is to viticulture in the Southern Rhône, as it doesn't come from France. Grenache originates from Spain (or possibly Sardinia) and is still grown widely in Spanish regions such as Rioja, Gredos Mountains and Priorat, where it's known as Garnacha. It's well suited to southern France, however, as it's a variety that likes hot, dry conditions. The grapes generate ample amounts of sugar as they ripen, which converts to generous amounts of alcohol (usually around 15%); along with the natural glycerol content in the grapes, Grenache produces full-bodied wines that are lush in texture. Wines made from pure Grenache (unusual but not unheard of here) tend to be ruby red in colour rather than purple like Syrah, and the flavours are typically more red fruited: strawberry, raspberry, plum. Other common aromas are dried Provence herbs (sometimes referred to as *garrigue* herbs) and rose petals.

Mourvèdre

Mourvèdre is another imported grape; it was more common further south in Provence until it made its way to the Rhône, but it originates – again – from Spain. It's another grape that needs hot weather in order to ripen fully, but unlike Grenache, it likes having easy access to water. It produces dense, dark wines that are more tannic than

Grenache – so it complements it well when blended. It has an earthier aromatic palette, with blackberry and sometimes leather or truffle notes as it ages.

Carignan

Carignan

Carignan has long been seen as a second-class grape variety – a workhorse that gives big crops of rustic wine. But lately it's been finding more fans – it performs well in very hot, dry conditions and contributes colour, acidity and tannin to the blend – all of which can be on the low side with Grenache. It's the third-most-planted grape in the Southern Rhône and like so many other grapes in this part of the Rhône, it's originally from Spain.

Cinsault

Cinsault

Another grape that was until recently unfairly maligned, Cinsault – a French grape through and through – is making a gradual comeback. It produces big, juicy grapes that add a certain fluidity to a blend and ripens at relatively low alcohol levels, so can help temper Grenache's natural tendency towards booziness. It has aromatic redcurrant, raspberry and cherry blossom notes and very fine tannins. Makes great rosé too.

Other red grapes you might come across in various corners of the Southern Rhône: Marselan, Counoise,

Muscat à Petits Grains Noirs, Caladoc, Gamay, Muscardin, Piquepoul Noir, Vaccarèse, Pinot Noir, Terret Noir, Couston, Calitor, Vidoc...

Southern Rhône white grapes

Grenache Blanc

There are even more white- and pink-skinned varieties than red ones in the south. Most of them go into white and rosé wines, of course, but some producers blend a small amount of white grapes into the reds to add freshness and interest.

Grenache Blanc

Like the Pinot grape family found further north in Burgundy and Alsace (Pinot Noir, Pinot Gris, Pinot Blanc), Grenache comes in three colours too – Grenache Noir (usually just called Grenache), Grenache Gris and Grenache Blanc. Grapes like to naturally mutate like this in vineyards, so it's no surprise to find so much Grenache Blanc used for white wines in the Southern Rhône. It doesn't have a strong character itself – it's full-bodied, usually with some subtle apple and pear aromas – but does a good job of binding together all the elements in a blend.

Clairette

Clairette

Clairette Blanche, to give it its full name, is similar to Grenache Blanc – it's full-bodied, with only moderate acidity – but it has a bit more flavour and character. It tends to have a good sense of freshness, with floral notes, aniseed and grapefruit. Wines based around Clairette (and it's pink-skinned sibling, Clairette Rose) can age surprisingly well.

Rolle

Rolle

This grape is better known by its Italian name Vermentino. It's mostly planted in the Luberon, but is gradually spreading further afield, gaining fans thanks to its brisk, zesty freshness.

Bourboulenc

If you've never been to the Rhône before, you probably haven't heard of Bourboulenc – it isn't grown anywhere else. It's a useful grape as it tends to offer some zesty citrus flavour and acidity, bringing freshness to blends.

Winemaking trends: Natural wine

Organic viticulture is growing in the Rhône; 20% of Rhône Valley vineyards are now certified organic. Biodynamic farming isn't so well known, but it's increasingly adopted by top wine estates. Based on the teachings of Rudolf Steiner, it views the farm as a self-sustaining ecosystem. Practitioners seek to optimize soil health and biodiversity, they eschew chemicals and work according to the phases of the moon. A more recent development is Natural wine. It doesn't have a precise definition, but Natural winemakers work organically or biodynamically, and attempt to make wine with as few processes, manipulations or additions as possible. It's a challenging way of working, as there is no recourse to using additives (such as tartaric acid or gum arabic) if the growing season doesn't go to plan – and when does it? The two hotspots of Natural winemaking in the Rhône Valley are on the west bank in the Southern Rhône, and in Saint-Joseph in the Northern Rhône. Some wine lovers embrace this style, believing it's a more authentic, warts-and-all rendition of a vineyard. Other wine lovers avoid it, having been discouraged by poor quality examples with off-flavours. The best, from addresses such as Domaine Saladain, can be vibrant, beautiful, emotional bottles. The bad ones can be pretty stinky.

Other white grapes you can find around the Southern Rhône include Ugni Blanc, Muscat à Petits Grains Blancs, Clairette Rose, Grenache Gris, Piquepoul Blanc, Chardonnay, Aligoté, Carignan Blanc, Macabeu, Piquepoul Gris, Picardan, Floréal…

Bourboulenc

Vintages

How much do vintages matter in the Rhône Valley? Not as much as they used to. Until the 1980s, it was common to have a few years every decade that suffered from poor weather, disease or other problems resulting in a poor quality crop. As winemaking skill and knowledge has increased – and the climate has become hotter – poor vintages are much rarer today. You'd have to go back to the biblical floods of 2002 to come across a really bad vintage (though 2008 wasn't brilliant either).

That said, every vintage delivers wines with an identifiably different profile, bestowing a certain personality to the wines made that year – whether it's lean and fresh, warm and mellow or tight and tannic, for example. Certain years might excel for white wines instead of red; others will be better in the Northern Rhône than the south. And, if you're looking for wines to keep, some vintages have longer lifespans than others. (Certain appellations are reliably long-lived, particularly Gigondas, Châteauneuf, Hermitage and Côte-Rôtie.)

So if you're presented with a number of different vintages of the same wine to choose from, the main question to ask yourself is this: am I in the mood for something young, juicy and energetic? Or do I feel like drinking a wine with a more developed, mellow, dusky flavour profile?

2023

A very decent year – ripe and juicy reds, particularly in Côte-Rôtie. Very good white wines.

2022

A very hot, dry year which produced good wines in a spread of styles – some reds are quite light; others are much more concentrated, with tough tannins. Not as good for whites, which can be a bit overripe.

Vineyards of Ampuis

2021

Like much of France, the Rhône Valley was hit by a hard spring frost, followed by a cool growing season. A great year for whites, in a lean, crisp style. Less good for reds; some are enjoyably fresh, but others lack concentration. Drink the reds young.

2020

An excellent year throughout the Rhône Valley, in both red and white.

2019

A year that saw the hottest temperatures on record in the Rhône; it was very dry too. The best wines (particularly around Côte-Rôtie and Châteauneuf) are exceptional, and will be very long-lived. But some wines can be overripe and jammy. Surprisingly vigorous white wines for a hot year, but time to drink most of them up now.

2018

A damp spring followed by a hot summer made for soft and sunny red wines that are best drunk sooner rather than later.

2017

Savoury reds with quite firm tannins that are softening up now, and will be long-lived. Particularly tannic in the Southern Rhône. Good whites.

2016

An exceptional vintage in the Southern Rhône – vibrant but opulent reds that will be best drunk from 2028, then last for a long time. Also very good in the Northern Rhône, albeit in a slightly less powerful style, that are drinking well now. Very good whites too.

2015

Extremely concentrated in the Northern Rhône; leave them until 2030. Lovely, juicy, opulent reds in the south that will be drinkable earlier. All but the best whites (essentially Hermitage, Châteauneuf) should have been drunk by now.

2014

A cooler, wetter year made for light reds that are best finished up now. Excellent whites, however, most of which are still good, and the best of which will be very long-lived.

2013

A late vintage with plenty of acidity and tannin – mixed quality, but the best are starting to drink well now, and will continue to do so for many years.

2012

A lovely year for reds, consistently good in the north and south, in a balanced and easy-going style.

2011

A season hampered by rains, making for fairly soft wines, most of which should have been finished by now. North better than south; white better than red.

2010

An excellent year – at least it will be, when the wines are finally ready to drink. Most are starting to soften up now, but some (like Hermitage) are still tough. Great concentration and power. Great whites as well as reds.

2009

Another very good year, but not as tannic as 2010, so drink the 2009s first – they're all about delicious, rich, generous fruit. Better in reds than whites.

14 of the greatest wines of the Rhône Valley

Château Rayas, Beaucastel, the La Las, Clos des Papes… these are names that resonate through the ages. Here we list 14 wines without which no Rhône lover's cellar is complete.

Southern Rhône

Château Rayas Châteauneuf-du-Pape 2009

Hidden in the woods near the village of Châteauneuf-du-Pape, Château Rayas is one of the most revered and mysterious estates in the Rhône Valley. It was established in 1880 by Albert Reynaud at the age of 45 after he went deaf. It's now run by his great-grandson Emmanuel Reynaud and his two sons. He owns three estates around the Southern Rhône: Château Rayas, Château de Fonsalette to the north of Châteauneuf and Château des Tours near Vacqueyras. All of his wines are worth seeking out (though they aren't open for visits) and have a similar house style. The jewel in the crown, however, is Château Rayas, a pure Grenache with spellbinding aromas of strawberry, rose, blood orange and herbs that despite – or perhaps because of? – its delicacy, can live for decades.

Château de Beaucastel Châteauneuf-du-Pape 'Hommage à Jacques Perrin' 2001

The Perrin family own various domaines and brands throughout the Rhône and further afield. Their most famous property is Château de Beaucastel which is situated at the north-eastern edge of Châteauneuf-du-Pape and dates back to 1549. The Perrins bought it relatively recently, in 1909. Always ahead of the curve, they were pioneers of organic, then biodynamic, viticulture. They were also one of the first to establish large plantings of Mourvèdre, and their top red is named after the visionary ancestor that embraced this variety. It contains around 80% old vine Mourvèdre, and produces a wine of baroque grandeur and complexity.

Clos des Papes Châteauneuf-du-Pape 2009

With over 400 years of family winemaking history, and 23 plots planted with all 18 permitted varieties, few people know Châteauneuf-du-Pape as well as Vincent Avril. His blending skills are second to none; he brings all this together to produce just a single red Châteauneuf and a single white, both of which are consistently among the most elegant expressions of what can be a forbidding style of wine. Both colours age very well indeed, and take on layers of complex flavours as they do.

Château de Saint Cosme Gigondas 'Le Poste' 2010

If Gigondas is now considered in many ways the equal of Châteauneuf-du-Pape, this is partly down to Louis Barruol, one of the most dynamic and consequential winemakers in the Rhône Valley. He's the president of the Gigondas appellation, and has established the family property as one of the leading estates in the Rhône since he took it over in 1992. He's best known for his three single-vineyard Gigondas cuvées: Le Poste, Le Claux and Hominis Fides. All are made from organically farmed old-vine Grenache, and all are equally brilliant. Le Poste, from a vineyard of limestone marl next to an 11th-century chapel, is a personal favourite, making ethereal reds and whites of rare purity and elegance.

Domaine Gourt de Mautens 2015

Gourt de Mautens isn't as easy to find as the finest Châteauneuf-du-Papes, but this biodynamic estate is a firm favourite among dedicated Rhône lovers. It belongs to Jérôme Bressy, who likes to use a large proportion of lesser-known local varieties in his wines, and for this reason his wine isn't bottled under a famous appellation. His wines are nonetheless among the top tier in the Rhône Valley. His reds are potent, concentrated, with a deep resonance and great capacity to age. His whites are richly full-bodied, with luxurious, waxy textures.

Northern Rhône

Domaine Jean-Paul Jamet Côte-Rôtie 'Côte Brune' 2016

Domaine Jamet was established in 1950 by Joseph Jamet; his sons, Jean-Paul and Jean-Luc, joined him in the 1970s. They parted ways in 2013 to set up their own operations. Jean-Paul stuck to a very traditional recipe, and most of his Côte-Rôtie vines are blended together to produce his unnamed *cuvée classique*, which is consistently one of the best wines in the appellation. He does make one single-vineyard wine every year, however, from an exceptional site called La Côte Brune. It produces a complete and harmonious wine that combines fruits, flowers, herbs and spices to electrifying effect, and is not just one of the best wines in the Rhône, but one of the finest wines in the world.

Domaine Yves Gangloff Côte-Rôtie 'La Barbarine' 2019

Increasingly hard to find – but worth tracking down – are Yves Gangloff's Côte-Rôties. This small estate has developed a cult following over the past decade, and on tasting the wines, it's not hard to see why. Yves, who has the style and charisma of an ageing rock star, manages to coax out an extraordinary elegance from these hillsides, making wines with the texture of the finest fur. He makes two Côte-Rôties: La Barbarine and La Sereine Noire. Both are beautiful; the main difference is that the vines are older in La Sereine Noire and it has stronger oak influence – so wait a little longer than La Barbarine before you open it.

Guigal Côte-Rôtie 'La Landonne' 2016

Guigal is one of the largest and most successful wine companies in the Rhône Valley. They own several properties dotted around the Rhône Valley, but they are most famous for their single vineyard Côte-Rôties, informally known as the 'La Las': 'La Landonne', 'La Mouline', 'La Turque' – soon to be joined by 'La Reynarde'. All of them undergo very long ageing in small new oak barrels – 42 months, in fact; much longer than their neighbours. The result is wines with a real wow-factor – Côte-Rôties in their red-carpet finery. 'La Mouline' is petite and aromatic and drinks well young; 'La Turque' is deep and spicy; 'La Landonne' is dark and savoury and needs some time in bottle before showing its best.

Domaine Georges Vernay Condrieu 'Coteau de Vernon' 2021

There is no name more closely associated with the appellation of Condrieu than Georges Vernay. After World War II, these slopes were almost abandoned, but Vernay rallied the remaining winegrowers and ensured Condrieu's survival. At the time, it was the only place in the world you could find the Viognier grape, so it was nearly lost; today, it's cultivated all over the world. It's a highly distinctive variety; its opulent texture and aromas of peach and jasmine can be too much for some people. But when grown on the Coteau de Vernon, it has a freshness, salinity and inner steel that gives it balance, drinkability and ageability.

Château-Grillet 2014

Rather like Beyoncé or Ronaldo, there are certain wines that go by a single name. Château-Grillet is the estate; their top wine is called Château-Grillet; the appellation is... you've guessed it... Château-Grillet. It's a tiny, ancient estate nestled in a south-facing, steep amphitheatre within the heart of the larger appellation of Condrieu. The style is similar – pure Viognier, floral, voluptuous and hedonistic – but it has a particular intensity that marks it out as something special.

Domaine Jean-Louis Chave Hermitage 1990

One of the most incredible things about the Rhône Valley is how long some estates have remained in the same family. Take Domaine Jean-Louis Chave, for example – the estate has been handed down from one generation to the next since 1481. They started out making wine in Saint-Joseph, but now they're best known for their Hermitage. They are one of the few family estates to own prime vineyards here, and they make the quintessential expression of this sacred hill. Their red Hermitage typically hits its stride at around 20 years of age; their white Hermitage is just as long-lived.

Chapoutier Ermitage 'L'Ermite' 2020

Is it Hermitage or Ermitage? Unusually, you can spell it either way; both are permitted. Chapoutier is one of the largest wine businesses in the Rhône, and it owns more land on this special hill than anyone else. Rather than blending all its different parcels of vines together, it produces a suite of single-vineyard Hermitage wines, three white and four red. It's hard to pick a favourite, but its white expression of the Ermite vineyard at the top of the hill is never less than thrilling – a particularly tense, energetic and focused style of white Hermitage that lasts forever.

Domaine Clape Cornas 2010

Once considered a poor cousin to Hermitage and Côte-Rôtie, Cornas is now beginning to get the recognition it deserves. The Clape family have one of the oldest estates in the village, and they capture the wild, wilful, thunderous nature of this jagged granite slope better than anyone. They have enviable parcels of old vines in the best plots, and faithfully stick to a traditional recipe to make wines of huge presence and texture. Very Old World, distinctly old school, deeply satisfying.

Domaine Thierry Allemand Cornas 'Reynard' 2019

While the Clape family are one of the most established winemaking families in Cornas, the Allemand family are relatively new to making wine. Thierry Allemand didn't come from a winemaking family, but learned his trade from local legend Robert Michel, and acquired his first vineyard in 1982. He now has 5ha, and is in the process of passing the reins over to his son Théo. They make two principal Cornas cuvées: 'Chaillots' is from their young vines, 'Reynard' is the old-vine cuvée. While both are expressive, aromatic and vigorous, Reynard typically has a little more depth and concentration.

Châteauneuf-du-Pape: hospitality with a mission

In the history of wine, there is no equivalent to Châteauneuf-du-Pape. This great appellation attracts visitors from around the world to its vineyards, and its wines are objects of fascination, even adoration. But Châteauneuf-du-Pape has never become insular or 'Disneyfied' – we're proud of our open sense of hospitality that keeps people at its core.

La Vinothèque – The wine hub

At the heart of the Châteauneuf-du-Pape wine tourism experience is La Vinothèque, a dynamic cultural and tasting space created by the winemakers' association. Housed in a beautifully restored former cellar, this venue represents the beating heart of the appellation's collective spirit. In the old papal town's ramparts, La Vinothèque offers visitors more than just wine – it's a gateway to understanding what makes Châteauneuf-du-Pape truly unique.

Your journey of discovery starts with a 45-minute discovery tasting (€25) led by a professional sommelier. In an ideal introduction to the region's style and diversity,

you'll taste five emblematic wines (four reds and one white). For those who wish to go deeper, La Vinothèque also hosts prestige tastings that explore the nuances of vineyard plots, winemaking techniques and ageing choices (60 minutes, €40).

Other specialized sessions include sensory tastings (€35), vertical or horizontal tastings and specially tailored masterclasses (available on request). Each expertly guided – and convivial – tasting will deepen your understanding of wine.

This unique approach reflects the broader philosophy of Châteauneuf-du-Pape – a region that resists standardization and embraces character, individuality and the slow pleasures of discovery. La Vinothèque is more than just a tasting room: it's a cultural hub where education, heritage and enjoyment converge.

The village also hosts numerous seasonal events such as Les Printemps de Châteauneuf-du-Pape, a springtime wine fair, or La Fête de la Veraison, a medieval-style celebration held each August. Châteauneuf-du-Pape offers unforgettable moments to wine lovers and the wine-curious alike.

In a world where everyone's in a hurry, Châteauneuf-du-Pape is a haven where every glass tells a story and every visit creates a lasting connection.

For more information and booking visit chateauneuf.com

Content supported by Châteauneuf-du-Pape

Appellations

What is an appellation?

The French wine appellation scheme was originally developed in the 1930s to stop winemakers from other regions fraudulently passing off their inferior wines as Châteauneuf-du-Pape (see p18). It has since been adopted all over France, and more broadly throughout Europe, not just for wine but for other food and agricultural products. Its full name is the *appellation d'origine contrôlée* (AOC) or *appellation d'origine protégée* (AOP) system (in English it's Protected Designation of Origin, or PDO). At the time of writing, there were 363 AOC wines in France.

Châteauneuf-du-Pape

In the Rhône, like in other regions, there are a number of different layers to the 'appellation pyramid'. The largest appellation is the loosest: AOC Côtes-du-Rhône wines accounts for nearly half of all the AOC wine produced in the Rhône Valley. It covers the largest area and has the least stringent rules of production around things like yields. Next up is AOC Côtes-du-Rhône Villages; then come the 21 AOC Côtes-du-Rhône Villages with Geographic Designation – or Named Villages for short. At the top of the pyramid are the 18 Crus, amounting to just 17% of all the AOC wine made in the Rhône Valley. These are the most famous appellations; they have the tightest rules of production and tend to be where the best wines are made.

There are, however, some other appellations that lie outside the main Côtes-du-Rhône growing area, officially called 'Other Rhône Valley' AOCs. And that's not to mention IGP wines or Vin de France! Let's take a look at them in turn so you know what to expect.

The 18 Crus

Southern Crus

Châteauneuf-du-Pape

The original AOC, the mothership, the heart of the Southern Rhône... even people that don't drink wine have heard of Châteauneuf-du-Pape. It helps that the name describes its story: 'the new castle of the pope' (see p16). And having your product approved by God's representative on Earth is, well, a godsend. This is the largest Cru in the Rhône Valley, and it makes the most powerful wines in the region – in both red and white – which is one factor that makes them so ageworthy. Many of the greatest wines of the Rhône Valley come from Châteauneuf.

For such a famous name, the village is surprisingly small. Until fairly recently, there was little of interest here, but significant investment and renovation over the past decade have transformed it. It's now home to an excellent hotel with a Michelin-starred restaurant (La Mère Germaine), several other very good places to eat and drink, and there are a number of top estates you can visit based in the village. If you're looking for somewhere smaller and less gridlocked than Avignon to use as a base, consider Châteauneuf.

Gigondas

One of the prettiest villages in the region also makes some of its best wine – Gigondas might be too small for a long stay, but it should be top of your list for places to visit. Positioned on the western edge of the Dentelles de Montmirail massif, the terroir here is completely different to Châteauneuf; the wines are correspondingly distinct. Though typically generous in style, they have a certain fresh, upright nature thanks to the altitude and limestone soils – and can age just as long. There is a choice of different places to eat to suit different budgets, and a few good options to stay – some just outside the village itself. White wine is relatively new to the appellation, successfully combining generosity and freshness.

Vacqueyras

A vast plateau of pebbles at the foot of the Dentelles de Montmirail, the reds of Vacqueyras are quintessentially

Gigondas

Southern Rhône: muscular, hearty, with concentrated forest berry fruits. Its sandy fringes make some of the best whites in the region too. It helps that this is home to some excellent producers and talented winemakers. The ancient village of Vacqueyras and neighbouring Sarrians are worth a quick wander on the way to the vineyards.

Rasteau
Rasteau Vin Doux Naturel

Rasteau is a pleasant village surrounded by vineyards, rising up into the wooded hills beyond. Their wines are particularly assertive, with very ripe and potent fruit flavours coupled with elegant textures. Before they made dry reds here, they were famous for their sweet wines made primarily from Grenache; mostly red, but they come in all three colours. Very little sweet wine is made today, but the tradition is still kept alive, thankfully, as they can be delicious on their own or with desserts.

Cairanne

A small village with a decent restaurant (La Tourne au Verre), Cairanne shares a border with Rasteau – but the wines are quite different. The reds tend to be a little less big and bold in style, more measured; less immediate impact perhaps, but with more elegance and drinkability. Unlike Rasteau, they also make white wine here, which can be among the most graceful in the Southern Rhône.

Vinsobres

The most northerly of the Southern Rhône Crus, Vinsobres is also one of the most recent to be promoted to the top of the quality pyramid. They only make red wines in this appellation, often with a generous dollop of Syrah, which gives good results here. The northerly location, elevation and wind currents that whistle in from the mountains produce wines with a good sense of freshness.

Beaumes de Venise rouge Muscat de Beaumes de Venise

Beaumes de Venise

Beaumes de Venise is a charming village at the southern point of the Dentelles de Montmirail. It's most famous for its honeyed sweet wine, mostly white, made from Muscat grapes, which have been grown here for 2,000 years. More recently, the village has been granted the appellation for dry red wines too, most of which are made further up in the mountains behind the village. The highest altitude vineyards create elegant, medium-bodied wines, and there are some more robust examples too.

Lirac

Lirac is just over the river from Châteauneuf-du-Pape, but the wines are more medium-bodied, elegant and refined with an energetic, brisk manner. Of the three Crus on the west bank of the Rhône, it's the most diverse, a grouping of four small villages, making very good wines in all three colours.

Tavel

Rosé only

Tavel is one of the oldest appellations in France, ratified just one day after Châteauneuf-du-Pape. It's unique among the appellations of the Rhône Valley in that it only makes rosé. They were once highly sought after, but fell out of fashion as the trend for very pale, Provençal rosé took over the world in the 2010s. The best are still appreciated by those in the know, who love their intensity, flavour, food-friendliness and ageability. Rosé with character made from a pretty village that's worth the detour.

Tavel

Laudun

Red and white

Most Crus start out on lower levels of the appellation pyramid then get promoted – Laudun is the most recent Cru to be established, from the 2024 vintage. It's historically famous for the quality of its white wines: nearly a third of the production here is white, much more than the other southern Crus. Take a walk up above the village of Laudun to explore the Roman ruins of Caesar's Camp, which offers views of the vineyards below.

Northern Crus

Côte-Rôtie

Red only

Côte-Rôtie is something of a non-sequitur; it means 'roasted slope' in English, but – although very warm – it's far from the hottest site in the Rhône. It's a band of vertiginous terraced vineyards that emerge from the Rhône, making for some of the most visually arresting agricultural land in the world. It has traditionally been the most northerly point that Syrah will ripen, giving a haunting, tender style of wine with

Côte-Rôtie

aromas of violet, raspberry and blackberry. The best are among the most elegant, complex and beautiful wines in the world. Ampuis might not be as picturesque as the villages of Provence, but if eating, drinking, buying wine and visiting wineries is your thing, then there will be enough to keep you entertained here for a day or so.

Condrieu

White only

Next door to Côte-Rôtie, on similarly extraordinary granite slopes, the white wines of Condrieu couldn't be more different. This is the original home of the Viognier grape, which naturally produces flamboyant, exotic, highly aromatic wines that brim with apricot, peach and jasmine flavours – highly distinctive, and adored by many. While the appellation of Condrieu extends southwards, the village of Condrieu itself is a useful overnight stop – it has a couple of hotels and a few places to eat.

Château-Grillet

White only

This is the odd one out – Château-Grillet is a single wine estate, small but ancient, at the heart of the Condrieu appellation. Thanks to a quirk of history, it has its own appellation. It also makes wines from pure Viognier, and they are highly sought-after, attracting very high prices. They don't accept visitors, but you can find their wines in some local restaurants.

Saint-Joseph

Red and white

Saint-Joseph is a long, thin appellation that runs down the west bank of the Rhône, connecting the northern and southern pole of the Northern Rhône. Rather than a specific village, Saint-Joseph is a succession of granite slopes, either made with pure Syrah for reds, or Marsanne, Roussanne or both grapes blended together for whites. It's home to some of the best value wines in the Northern Rhône.

Cornas

Red only

At the southern point of Saint-Joseph lies Cornas; the town has a bakery and a church but not a lot else. Behind it, however, you can't help but spot a rumpled amphitheatre of granite that's covered in vines. This is home to some of the wildest, most untamed and wonderfully visceral expressions of the Syrah grape.

Saint-Péray

White only

At the start of the 20th century, 90% of Saint-Péray was sparkling; now 90% is still. Either way, they only make whites here, from Marsanne, Roussanne or both. The sparkling wines are fuller in body than Champagne, and can be very pleasant; the whites are medium- to full-bodied and can be really lovely: soft, generous and fresh. Stop in the village for a day or so – it's only small, but there are good options for lunch and dinner, shopping for wine, visiting wineries and walking.

Hermitage

Red and white

To understand the French notion of terroir, all you need to do is stand on the riverbank in the village of Tournon and cast your eyes over the river to the hill of Hermitage. You can see why this site is so magical: the slope angles the vines towards the sun; it faces south, so the vines are sheltered from the wind, each supported by a wooden stake. What you don't see is the multiple types and ages of rock beneath, or the care that goes into tending these plants. It all adds up to some of the most majestic, long-lived red and white wines in France. At the foot of the hill is the village of Tain l'Hermitage, which contains everything a food and wine lover needs to keep them occupied. Over the bridge on the opposite bank, Tournon is larger and prettier, but they are two sides of the same coin. Either one offers the ideal base to explore the vineyards of the Northern Rhône.

Crozes-Hermitage
Red and white

The biggest appellation in the Northern Rhône surrounds the little hill of Hermitage, stretching north, east and mostly south of Tain l'Hermitage. There are pockets of excellent terrain here, and the appellation produces many delicious red and white wines, albeit not on the same scale as Hermitage. This was once all apricot trees, and now has vines as far as the eye can see.

Côtes du Rhône Villages

AOC Côtes-du-Rhône comprises 172 villages; the best 95 of these villages can use the appellation AOC Côtes-du-Rhône Villages if they stick to stricter rules – so (in theory at least) it represents a step up in quality.

There are 21 villages that are allowed to add their name to the appellation: AOC Côtes-du-Rhône Villages Sablet, for example. These 'Named Villages' are another step up in the appellation pyramid, with even more stringent rules of production. When a village is promoted to a Cru, this is the pool from which they are chosen. As such, most are striving for quality, but are as yet unable to charge Cru-level prices – so this is often where to look for the best value bottles.

They are dotted all over the Southern Rhône, and are as

follows: Chusclan, Gadagne, Massif d'Uchaux, Nyons, Plan de Dieu, Puyméras, Roaix, Rochegude, Rousset-les-Vignes, Sablet, Saint-Andéol, Sainte-Cécile, Saint-Gervais, Saint-Maurice, Saint-Pantaléon-les-Vignes, Séguret, Signargues, Suze-la-Rousse, Vaison-la-Romaine, Valréas and Visan. Some are large, some tiny; all make red, some make white and rosé too. They all have their charms.

Some particularly pretty villages include Sablet, Sainte-Cécile, Séguret, Suze-la-Rousse, Vaison-la-Romaine and Visan.

Côtes-du-Rhône

By far the largest appellation, Côtes-du-Rhône is a name that's recognized the world over. Though largely associated with red wine, white wine now amounts to 8% (and growing) and it's the same amount for rosé. Though not all Côtes-du-Rhônes will make an indelible mark on your memory, most will pleasurably wash down a burger or pair admirably with the TV series you're currently bingeing.

It might be the biggest appellation, but don't assume that Côtes-du-Rhône always means average quality – there are pockets of exceptional terroir here and there within the larger growing area that can make very good wines in the right hands.

Satellite appellations

Circling the central Côtes-du-Rhône growing area is a collection of 'other Rhône Valley' appellations – they sit within the Rhône family but don't have 'Rhône' in their appellation names. Generalizing is impossible; some are vast, some are minute. Here's a brief idea of what to expect:

Costières de Nîmes – a large appellation of pebbly soils that spreads close to the Mediterranean and enjoys its cooling sea breezes. Lots to see and do, from the Camargue estuary to the Roman city of Nîmes.

Clairette de Bellegarde – Bellegarde is a single village at the heart of Costières de Nîmes; when they make pure white Clairette here, the results can be lovely and deserve their own appellation.

Uzès

Duché d'Uzès – aromatic, medium-bodied whites and fresh Syrah-based reds from the higher spots in this large area that stretches from the Cevennes mountains to the Rhône river. Take a drive around some of its pretty villages, and don't miss the bohemian town of Uzès itself.

Côtes du Vivarais – in the Southern Rhône, this appellation represents the northernmost part of the west bank where the limestone Ardèche hills start to rise up. So much to see and do around here, particularly if you like activities like kayaking, caving and walking.

Grignan-les-Adhémar – the northernmost appellation on the east bank in the Southern Rhône, producing approachable reds, whites and rosés.

Ventoux – a titanic appellation: vineyards on the slopes of Mont Ventoux itself enjoy the freshness of altitude; those on the plains below enjoy a warmer climate among picturesque villages like Isle-sur-la-Sorgue, Pernes-les-Fontaines and Crillon-le-Brave. Pockets of exceptional terroir and plenty of winemaking talent make for some Cru-level wines – hunt them out!

Luberon – one of the most picturesque parts of the Rhône Valley, with countless pretty villages to explore: Bonnieux, Gourdes, Roussillon, Lourmarin... you could spend a week here exploring – and many do; it's popular with tourists. Elegant whites and fresh reds will keep you well watered.

The Diois – this is very different from the other seven satellites; it's almost a wine region in itself, containing four discrete appellations. It does grow some classically Rhône varieties, but the wines of the dramatic Drôme Valley are very different from what's found elsewhere. Most of the output is sweet, sparkling Clairette de Die; it also makes some dry sparkling called Crémant de Die. The whites, reds and rosés from tiny AOCs Clairette de Die and Châtillon-en-Diois are light-bodied and brisk, sometimes using varieties more associated with Burgundy (Chardonnay, Pinot Noir and Aligoté).

IGP and Vin de France

If you plant vines outside these appellations, or you want to grow varieties that aren't on the list of what's permitted, then nothing's stopping you – but you'll have to bottle your wines under a different label. One option is *Indication Géographique Protégée* (IGP), known as Protected Geographical Indication (PGI) in English. These are typically much bigger areas than AOCs, with much looser rules of production, giving winemakers more freedom to experiment. Another option is bottling wines under Vin de France – so there is no geographical designation stated on the label.

Drôme Valley

Rhône cuisine

Because of its size, the Rhône Valley doesn't have a unified cuisine. The Northern Rhône is closer to Lyon in terms of food; the Southern Rhône is more Provençal or Mediterranean in flavour.

Northern Rhône cuisine

Many visitors arrive in Lyon by plane or train to start their trip to the Rhône. And what better place than the capital of French gastronomy?

Lyon, the third-largest city in France after Paris and Marseille, is the meeting point of several French gastronomic cultures: poultry from Bresse, Charolais beef, fish and frogs from the Dombes, fruit and vegetables from the Drôme and Ardèche – and wine, of course: Savoie, Jura, Burgundy, Beaujolais and the Rhône. No wonder Lyon has one of the highest numbers of restaurants per capita in France.

Compared to the Southern Rhône, you're more likely to find plentiful pork products here: sausages, salami, trotters, ham, terrines and endless charcuterie such as the local *rosette de Lyon*. Potatoes too are more common, and so is butter and cream. If this sounds heavy, go for a salad – but maybe not a *salade lyonnaise*, as among the leaves you'll find a handful of lardons and a poached egg.

Andouillette, a large sausage made from the intestines of a pig, is a local speciality. It's an

Andouillette

Saint-Marcellin cheese

acquired taste: fans enjoy its ripe, earthy, piggy aromas; detractors say it smells like faeces. Production is overseen by the AAAAA – the *Association Amicale des Amateurs d'Andouillette Authentique* (The Friendly Club of Lovers of Authentic Andouillette).

Local cheeses include Saint-Félicien and Saint-Marcellin – soft and creamy cow's milk cheeses that are alike in style. These are produced close to Lyon, but as you work your way further south, goat's cheeses become more common, such as the little *rigotte de Condrieu*, which works well with the wine of the same name. It's not always obvious what to serve Condrieu with, as it's so rich and aromatic – but it's much more versatile than you might think, working with fish dishes, seafood, poultry… and it's excellent paired with roast pork and aromatic herbs. Côte-Rôtie is highly adaptable, working well with game birds and duck, but more powerful styles can also easily stand up to roast lamb or beef. Even the most robustly flavoured dishes won't trounce a powerful Cornas.

Hermitage is a perfect match for much high-level gastronomic cookery. For richly sauced fish dishes, or veal with cream sauces and wild mushrooms, go white; for game and unsauced red meats, choose a red. Crozes-Hermitage works better with less intensely flavoured food, and most are delicious by themselves – reds and whites.

Southern Rhône cuisine

The vineyards peter out after Saint Péray. It's hard to say exactly where you exit the Northern Rhône and enter the Southern Rhône, but you feel it when it happens; most people describe nougat kingdom Montélimar as the frontier. Suddenly the sun feels a little warmer, the landscape expands and tell-tale purple fields of lavender appear.

There are various specialities found in different corners of the region: cherries in Ventoux, strawberries in Carpentras, red rice in the Camargue. Olives are grown throughout; the meaty black Tanche olives from Nyons were

the first to be granted their own appellation. Don't miss the local wine too – Nyons is the most recent of the 21 Côtes-du-Rhône Named Villages.

Rosemary and thyme, sometimes described as *garrigue* herbs, grow so rampantly that you never need to buy them here. Their flavours work well with local goat's milk cheeses (the climate is too hot and dry to sustain pasture for cows). If you like it young and moist, ask for it *frais;* if you prefer a stronger taste and firmer texture, request it *affiné*. It works much better with white wines than reds.

White wine goes well with the local truffles too. These 'black diamonds' might be more commonly associated with Périgord in western France, but oak trees are common in the Southern Rhône and truffles (*tuber melanosporum*) are a booming business. They are in season from December to March, and if you're a fan of this perfumed fungus, don't miss the truffle market in Richerenches every Saturday while they're in season.

Fruit and vegetables in France are strictly seasonal. In the spring and summer months, markets are rich with fresh produce; certain items only appear for a few weeks before they disappear again for another year. The tomatoes, in particular, are superb. Vegetarians and vegans will find much to enjoy – particularly if self-catering. When working with fresh vegetables, it's hard to go wrong if you pair them with local whites and rosés. If using light spices, think Tavel.

The high temperatures and smoky flavours from cooking on grills and barbecues call for red wines: pork and veal with juicy, medium-bodied styles such as Ventoux or Lirac; for beef and game, choose full-bodied east bank Crus. If you've spotted a very old bottle on a wine list, keep it simple and avoid rich sauces and accompaniments.

But don't worry too much about nailing the perfect food and wine match – it's highly unlikely that choosing the 'wrong' wine is going to spoil your meal. The majority of neighbourhood restaurants will serve local dishes and offer local wines – often from the immediate vicinity – and the two tend to work together naturally. If in doubt, just ask the waiter which they would choose (only fine dining establishments will have a dedicated sommelier).

When it comes to serving red Rhône wines, there is one piece of advice that trumps all others: ensure they're cool – they taste much better fresh (around 16 to 18°C) than at room temperature. If your red is too warm, ask for an ice bucket.

Black truffles

Old vine at Domaine Famille Isabel Ferrando

Visiting the Rhône

There are marked differences between the Northern Rhône and the Southern Rhône. The sizzling south has long been a holiday destination for both national and international holidaymakers, so it has a well-developed travel and tourism network. There are countless activities to suit all tastes and all ages, on top of a food and wine scene that can amply entertain even the most gluttonous.

Vineyards of the Diois

The Northern Rhône offers a different type of holiday. It has its fair share of visitors, but it's not as geared up for tourism; whether that's a good or bad thing depends on the experience you seek. It's not as picturesque as the south, and it has fewer attractions and activities for children. But its landscapes are stunning, it's not as scorchingly hot in summer and there are fewer crowds.

If you're a dedicated wine lover, the choice will likely be driven by your preferred style of wine – if you collect Châteauneuf or go weak at the knees for Northern Rhône Syrah, the choice will be clear.

Getting there

If you're just exploring the north, Lyon is the obvious starting point. Grenoble Isère Airport is 90 minutes' drive away; Lyon Saint-Exupéry Airport to the centre of town takes less than an hour by car, or half an hour on the Rhônexpress tram. Lyon is easily accessible via the Eurostar from London by changing trains in Paris or Lille and taking a TGV to arrive in central Lyon at the Gare Part-Dieu.

If you're concentrating on the south, Marseille Provence is a good airport option, or Montpellier Méditerranée.

Getting around

Hiring a car is strongly recommended to explore the Southern Rhône. If you use Avignon as a base, there are local buses (reliable) and local trains (fairly reliable), but it's advisable to do some timetable research before you set off. If you want to visit wineries, a car will vastly open up your options. Taxis are inexplicably, eye-wateringly expensive. Exploring the Northern Rhône without a car would be even more challenging, but hiring bicycles from Tain l'Hermitage or Tournon could be an option. If you do hire a car, be aware that motorways charge tolls if you use them, and GPS systems and online maps are liable to send you on unsuitable dirt tracks through vineyards; stick to paved roads. And don't forget it's usually possible to hire a car in Marseille and drop it in Lyon (or vice versa) if you're exploring the whole valley.

When to visit

Not all attractions are open before May, but April and May are typically warm, sunny and not too crowded. July and August can get very hot in the Southern Rhône; temperatures over 35°C aren't uncommon, though over 40°C is rare. Most winemakers take August off, so if you want to visit wineries, avoid August. You might get lucky with the weather in October, but it's a gamble.

Where to base yourself

For the Northern Rhône, you could base yourself in Lyon; you'd never run out of restaurant options (see pp153-158). But to immerse yourself in the region, consider Tain l'Hermitage or Tournon. They face each other on either side of the Rhône, connected by a bridge. Tain has a busy road running through it, but either side is an option; you'll be passing between them most days anyway.

In the south, the city of Avignon is the obvious place to stay; it's right at the heart of the region, and is well connected by road and rail. More importantly, it's vibrant, buzzy and fun, with plenty to keep you engaged, including museums, theatres, restaurants, great independent shops and more.

If you'd prefer a small town or village – or you want to avoid the crowds and high prices during the Avignon Festival in July – there are other options. You could try Châteauneuf-du-Pape (see chapter on Appellations), or another small village in the central Vaucluse such as Gigondas or Cairanne. Other possibilities are the Luberon – Bonnieux, Lourmarin, Gourdes and Roussillon are all very pretty – but you're an hour's drive from Avignon. Or explore the lesser-known (but unspoilt and intriguing) Gard *département* on the west bank of the Rhône, basing yourself in the dreamy town of Uzès.

Festivals

Countless festivals take place throughout the Rhône Valley every year, from the huge to the personal, from wild to sedate – there's something for everyone.

From north to south:

Nuits Sonores is a festival of electronic and avant garde music held every year at the **end of May** in Lyon. For over 20 years, it's been bringing the cream of dance music talent together from Europe and beyond, and hosting them in venues across the city. Think Jeff Mills, Massive Attack, Autechre, Bicep… the line-ups are incredible.

Jazz à Vienne was created in 1981, and is still bringing the greatest jazz talent to Vienne every year in the **first half of July.** Its epicentre is the Théâtre Antique, which was built in the 1st century CE. It attracts over 200,000 visitors a

Jazz à Vienne

Avignon Festival

year, and two-thirds of the concerts are free. Previous acts include Ray Charles, James Brown, Herbie Hancock and Sting.

Avignon Festival – this is the big one – a huge arts festival that has been held every year in Avignon **throughout July** since 1947. This internationally respected celebration of contemporary performing arts typically comprises 45 large shows, most of which are original productions; the 'Festival Off' welcomes a further 1,000 companies to perform under their own initiative. Expect Avignon to be heaving with visitors in July, and for accommodation to be at a premium.

Markets

Who doesn't enjoy lazily wandering around the hubbub of local markets with the sun on your back? Most towns and villages will have a food market of decent size on a set day. There are some, however, which are worth travelling for.

From north to south:

Romans-sur-Isère, food, every Sunday morning.

They have markets most days in Romans, but the food one on Sunday is the best; bring your camera – it's very photogenic.

Isle-sur-la-Sorgue

Isle-sur-la-Sorgue, food, homewares and antiques, every Sunday morning.

One of the biggest and best markets in Provence in the lovely island village of Isle-sur-la-Sorgue. Lots of antique shops too.

Marché d'Apt, food, homewares and antiques, every Saturday morning.

The sizeable market in this pretty village has been held since the 12th century.

Marché d'Apt

Velleron, food, every evening except Sundays 6.00pm to 7.30pm from April to September; otherwise every Tuesday, Friday and Saturday between 4.30pm and 6pm.

The car-park setting is functional rather than pretty, but the produce here is sensationally good. It's where the locals go.

Richerenches, truffles, every Saturday morning from mid-November until the end of March.

Do you like truffles? There are hundreds of producers here, and it's easy to buy single truffles for personal use. There's even a truffle museum. Pack your truffle shaver!

Uzès, food, every Wednesday and Saturday morning.

Saturday is the more popular day, with numerous stalls with the best products from the region in picturesque surroundings.

Market tips

- Markets may be shut on certain public holidays, etc., so it's always worth checking to see whether it's happening before you travel.
- Get there as early as you can; too late, and you might have difficulty finding a parking spot and much of the best produce will have been snapped up.
- Book lunch in advance – nearby restaurants will be busy.
- Take shopping bags.

Uzès market

Things to do in the Northern Rhône

From north to south:

If you're looking for activities, Lyon is your best bet. You could lose yourself for days wandering around the various quarters of the **Presqu'île**. There are plenty of little wine bars, wine shops and bistros just north and northwest of the Place des Terreaux, for example.

Fourvière is another good option for whiling away an afternoon. Take the funicular railway. It has more in the way of ancient monuments and buildings to discover, such as the 19th-century Basilique Notre-Dame, a vast Roman stone amphitheatre and the 101m-tall Metallic Tower, which predates the Eiffel Tower. There are also some parks if you have children that need a run-around.

Fourvière

If you need even more space, visit the **Parc de la Tête d'Or,** the biggest urban park in France. Created in 1857, it has lots to keep little ones (and big ones) entertained, including a zoo, a boating lake, botanical gardens, a miniature railway and pony rides. And no trip to Lyon would be complete without a visit to food hall **Les Halles Paul Bocuse**. It's open all day, every day, and is a gastronaut's dream.

Once you've settled into your holiday vibe and are venturing south into the winelands, there are fewer tourist activities – entertainment becomes much more food-and-wine based. In Côte-Rôtie, however, you could take a walk along the

Parc de la Tête d'Or

Train de l'Ardèche

new **Belvedere Path** in Tupin-et-Semons for a lovely view of the vineyards. Further south, the **Train de l'Ardèche** departs from Saint-Jean-de-Muzols – it's a steam train and the route has spectacular views. It runs twice a day during summer months, and a round trip takes around 90 minutes. Great for young children; under 10s go free.

Chapelle Saint-Christophe

When you reach Tain l'Hermitage, take a walk up to the iconic **Chapelle Saint-Christophe** at the top of the hill of Hermitage. You can access it easily from the northern exit of the Place du Taurobole, and the walk up and down takes around 45 minutes if you don't stop. But you'll want to – the views are incredible. Take sturdy footwear, a bottle of Hermitage, stemless glasses and a corkscrew! Afterwards, visit the **Valrhona Cité du Chocolat** – take the full tour, or just stock up on fabulous chocolate products in the boutique.

Things to do in the Southern Rhône

Pont d'Arc

As you travel south into the Southern Rhône, it's worth spending some time in the **Ardèche** – particularly if you enjoy outdoor pursuits. There are countless companies in the village of Vallon Pont d'Arc offering activities for all ages and levels of ability – try **Face Sud**. For a more sedate afternoon, you could visit the breathtaking **Pont d'Arc** itself, a natural limestone arch over the river, but expect crowds. Another option is the **Grotte Chauvet**, a cave featuring some of the best-preserved figurative cave paintings in the world. In order to preserve it, you can't enter the original cave itself, but you can visit a perfect replica.

Grotte Chauvet

Travel south and you change département from the Ardèche to the Gard. Just outside Uzès you'll find the **Haribo Sweet Museum**, which is a godsend if you need to bribe your children while you visit winemakers. West of Avignon is the **Pont du Gard**, an ancient Roman aqueduct built in the 1st century CE – it's a staggering feat of human ingenuity, and you can even go for a swim in the river on a hot day. Eventually, as you approach the Mediterranean, you'll pass through the **Camargue**, a huge estuary with a culture and feel all of its own. Wild horses, bulls, pink flamingos... it's a memorable day out. Just remember to take insect repellent.

Camargue

If you were travelling down from the Northern Rhône on the east bank of the river, a good place to stop is **L'Essentiel de Lavande**, an organic flower farm to the east of Montélimar. You can order picnics in advance, watch distillation demonstrations or even have a massage. Fifteen kilometres further south is the **Château de Grignan**, a fortress built on a rocky promontory with 1,000 years of history. If ancient buildings are your passion, a further 15km south is the **Château de Suze la Rousse**, another imposing

Château de Grignan

Château de Suze la Rousse

Dentelles de Montmirail

castle that's now home to the Université du Vin. If wildlife is more your thing, try **La Ferme aux Crocodiles** in Pierrelatte, home to various reptiles, some terrifying, some cute.

Further east into the Vaucluse, there's plenty of good walking to do in the **Baronnies Regional Nature Park**, and in the **Dentelles de Montmirail**. For great views over the vineyards of the Vaucluse, contact the **Aéroclub de Plan de Dieu**. They offer discovery flights that are surprisingly affordable if shared between a few people. A special place to visit on foot is near the pretty village of Isle-sur-la-Sorgue; the **Fontaine de Vaucluse** is the mountainous source of the Sorgue river, a place with a distinctly mystical vibe.

Fontaine de Vaucluse

You could happily spend a relaxing week exploring the gorgeous villages of the **Luberon** and its markets. If you're based there, drop in to the **Ferme de Cabrières** in Lambesc, an organic fruit and herb farm, with activities for children if required. If you're looking for something more spectacular, look no further than **Les Carrières de Lumières** in Les Baux de Provence. It's a huge former quarry that's been repurposed to offer art-based multimedia shows, where they project images of famous paintings set to music. It really works!

Les Carrières de Lumières

Wine routes

Here are some options to get a good taste of the Northern and Southern Rhône. If you only have a few days in the south and a few in the north, you can just pick the days that appeal most. If you're planning a short trip, bear in mind that many wineries, especially in the Northern Rhône, don't accept visitors at weekends. And many restaurants in Lyon are closed at the weekends. It's puzzling, I know, but there we are. For details of restaurants, hotels and other venues, see The Guide starting on p114.

Tupin-et-Semons

These suggestions assume that you're able-bodied and have access to your own transport. If not, there are plenty of further options in The Guide in the second half of this book. Bear in mind that all restaurants and attractions can change their days and hours of opening unexpectedly, so always check websites or call to check that they will be open in advance. Booking is always advisable.

A week in the Northern Rhône

Day 1, Sunday: Arrival in Lyon

Morning

- Stay: Check in to **Villa Maïa** and take a minute to take in the view from the bar.
- Activity: Most shops are closed on Sundays, so walk up to the **Parc des Hauteurs** to the **Basilique Notre-Dame**, then over to the amphitheatres.

Afternoon

- Lunch: Visit a traditional bouchon lyonnais such as **Café Comptoir Abel**.

Basilique Notre-Dame

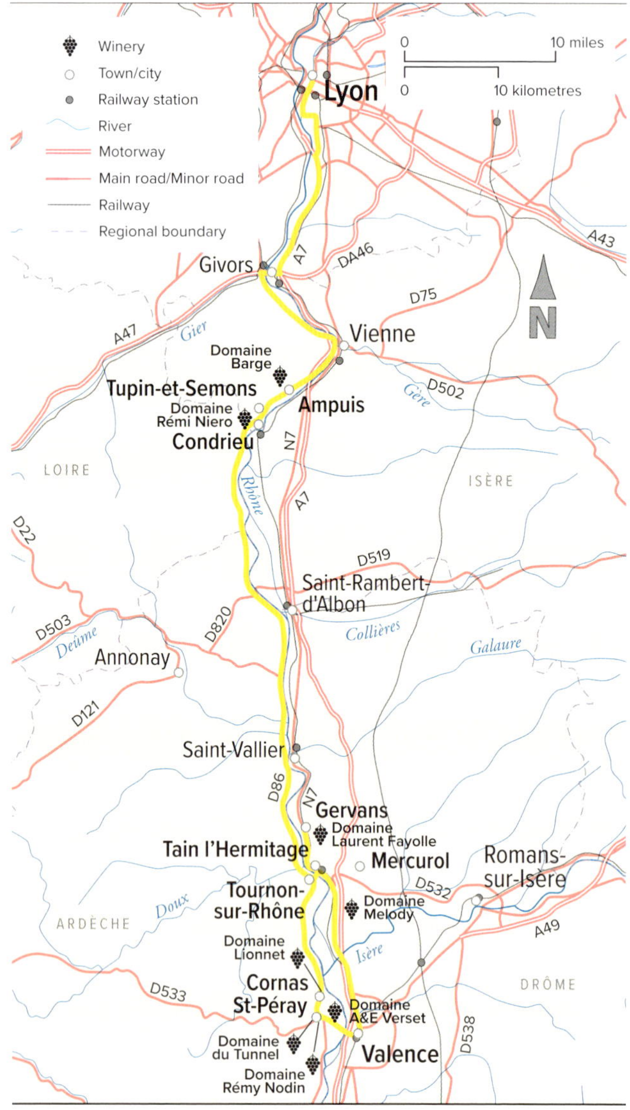
Winery
Town/city
Railway station
River
Motorway
Main road/Minor road
Railway
Regional boundary
0
10 miles
0
10 kilometres
Lyon
Givors
A7
DA46
A43
D75
A47
Gier
Vienne
Domaine Barge
Tupin-et-Semons
Domaine Rémi Niero
Ampuis
Gère
D502
Condrieu
N7
LOIRE
Rhône
A7
ISÈRE
D22
D519
Saint-Rambert-d'Albon
D503
Deûme
D820
Collières
Galaure
Annonay
D121
Saint-Vallier
D86
N7
Gervans
Domaine Laurent Fayolle
Tain l'Hermitage
Mercurol
Romans-sur-Isère
D532
Tournon-sur-Rhône
Domaine Melody
ARDÈCHE
Doux
A49
Domaine Lionnet
Isère
Cornas
DRÔME
D533
St-Péray
Domaine A&E Verset
D538
Domaine du Tunnel
Valence
Domaine Rémy Nodin

- Activity: Take a tram or bus to **Les Halles Paul Bocuse** and immerse yourself in this temple of French gastronomic delight. If the weather is good, take your haul to the **Parc du Tete d'Or** for a picnic, just 20 minutes away by foot.

Evening

- Dinner: You're unlikely to want a huge meal by this point, so visit **Le Dôme** at the **InterContinental Lyon – Hotel Dieu** for cocktails and snacks.

Day 2, Monday

Condrieu

Morning

- Activity: Visit **Domaine Barge** in Côte-Rôtie or **Domaine Rémi Niero** in Condrieu (see The Guide).

Afternoon

- Lunch: Informal lunch at **Les Epicurieux**. The walls are lined with bottles; it's a great selection that you can buy to drink in or take out. See if you can spot any winemakers!
- Activity: Follow the hairpin bends up the slopes to Tupin-et-Semons for the little Belvedere walk with views over the vineyards – selfies galore. Pop into **La Bouteillerie** in Condrieu to pick up some hard-to-find bottles.

Evening

- Dinner: If you want to drive back to Lyon before dining out, go to **Café Terroir** and dig into its excellent wine list. If you'd prefer a view of the vineyards, visit the refined **Les Gagères** in Tupin-et-Semons.

Tupin-et-Semons

Day 3, Tuesday

Morning

- Stay: Drive to Tournon, check in at the elegant **Hôtel de la Villeon**.
- Activity: Stock up on snacks in Tournon, then take a walk up the hillside of Saint-Joseph – follow signs for the Sentier des Tours and the Belvedère de la Chapelle.

Afternoon

- Lunch: Picnic with views across the river to the hill of Hermitage.
- Activity: Visit **Domaine Laurent Fayolle** or **Domaine Melody** in Crozes-Hermitage.

Evening

- Dinner: Sensitive, precise cooking and a deep understanding of the local wines makes **Les Mangevins** an unmissable place to eat.

Day 4, Wednesday

Morning

- Activity: Drive to Saint-Péray via Cornas – stop in the village of Cornas to take in the vineyards. Walk up to the ruins of the **Château de Crussol** in Saint-Péray.

Tournon and Tain l'Hermitage

Afternoon

- Lunch: **Auberge de Crussol** has a well-chosen list of local wines, an airy terrasse and varied cuts of meat cooked over fire.
- Activity: Visit **Domaine Rémy Nodin** or **Domaine du Tunnel** in Saint-Péray.

Evening

- Dinner: The husband-and-wife team at **Le Tournesol** in Tournon combine friendly service, an excellent, affordable wine list and delicious food.

Day 5, Thursday

Morning

- Activity: Stock up on bread and cheese (**La Fromagerie de Karine** in Tain is very good); pop into **Chapoutier's** boutique on Avenue Dr Paul Durand for a bottle of Hermitage, then make your way to the Chapelle Saint-Christophe.

Afternoon

- Lunch: Picnic with views across the river to Saint-Joseph and Saint-Péray. Take care on the way down – the ground can be slippery!
- Activity: Visit **Chapoutier** or **Delas** in Tain l'Hermitage.

Evening

- Dinner: You can find precise cooking and an excellent wine list at **Le Cerisier**.

Day 6, Friday

Morning

- Activity: Drive to Valence, take a wander around the **Parc Jouvet** or the **Musée de Valence**.

Afternoon

- Lunch: **Le Bac à Traille** or **La Cachette** are next door to each other; one is the bistro, the other is the Michelin-starred restaurant. Take your pick!
- Activity: Visit **Domaine Lionnet** or **Domaine A&E Verset** in Cornas.

Evening

- Dinner: If you chose the bistro for lunch, treat yourself to dinner at the epic three-star Michelin **Restaurant Pic**. If you'd prefer to return to Tournon before dining out, take a stroll over the footbridge to Tain and pop into **Le Bateau Ivre** for cheese and charcuterie and some local beers – if you can resist the temptation of their well-priced wine list.

Day 7, Saturday

Morning

- Activity: Check out of the hotel. If the siren call of Lyon shopping is irresistible, take the motorway. For a more leisurely, scenic drive, take the D86 – enjoy majestic views of the vineyards of Saint-Joseph all the way back to Ampuis.

Afternoon

- Lunch: If you took the motorway, have lunch at **Bouchon Tupin**. Otherwise, pop in to the winemaker-owned **Bistro de Serine** for lunch – excellent list of Côte-Rôtie and Condrieu, most of which are available from their wine shop next door.
- Activity: Check in to **Hôtel Globe et Cecil**; wander around the Presqu'île to satiate your shopping desires.

Evening

- Dinner: Go bar hopping around the wine bars of Les Terreaux: **Micro Sillon**, **Satriale**, **Odessa Comptoir**... ask the servers for more recommendations and you could be out all night.

Ampuis

A week in the Southern Rhône

Day 1, Sunday: Arrival in Marseille

Morning

- Stay: Drive to Avignon, check in to the 16th-century **Hôtel d'Europe**.
- Activity: Soak up the Provençal warmth on the streets of Avignon – stroll through the pedestrianized passageways on the way to lunch.

Afternoon

- Lunch: Rock up at the **Cabane d'Oléron**, essentially a shack tacked on to the back of Les Halles food halls. It's not much to look at, but the seafood is as fresh as can be.
- Activity: Wander through **Les Halles**, grab some edible goodies, wander back through the streets of Avignon past wine shop **Liquid** to pick up a few good bottles.

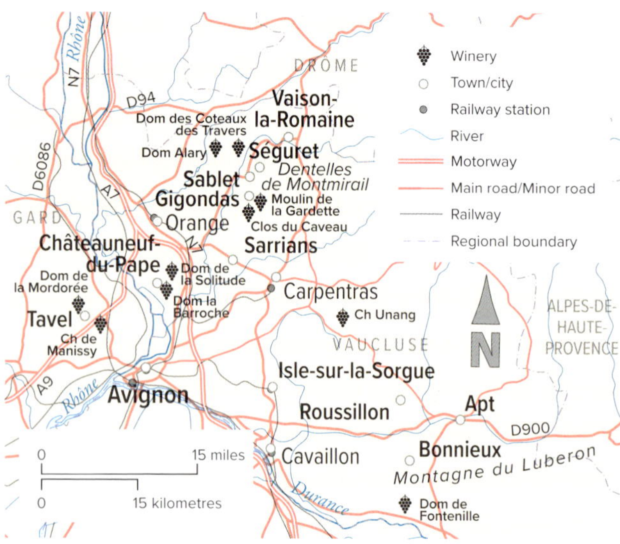

Evening

- Dinner: **La Mirande** is the grandest restaurant in Avignon. You deserve it.

Day 2, Monday

Morning

- Activity: Drive to Tavel, visit **Domaine de la Mordorée** or **Château de Manissy**.

Pont du Gard

Afternoon

- Lunch: Find a good bottle of Natural wine – preferably Tavel – to accompany your meal on the terrasse of **La Courtille**.
- Activity: Cast your eyes on the **Pont du Gard** and be flabbergasted at what humans can achieve.

Evening

- Dinner: Smart yet comfortable, **La Fourchette** never fails to satisfy with its traditional local cuisine and excellent service.

Day 3, Tuesday

Morning

- Activity: Drive to Châteauneuf-du-Pape, climb the alleyways up to the ruined château, take in the view and maybe enjoy an ice-cream.

Châteauneuf-du-Pape

Afternoon

- Lunch: **Le Verger des Papes** is just next door, which has an attractive terrasse with panoramic views and a good list of young Châteauneuf.
- Activity: Visit **Domaine la Barroche** or **Domaine de la Solitude**.

Evening

- Dinner: Don't miss a meal at **La Mère Germaine**; it's one of the best restaurants (and hotels) in the region. If you're heading back to Avignon, drop in to **Le 46** – it has a brilliant list of wines by the bottle and glass.

Day 4, Wednesday

Morning

- Stay: Check out of the hotel. Drive to Gigondas, check in to **Villa Sainte-Anne**.
- Activity: Walk up to the village itself, wander around the streets, up to the chapel. Pick up some picnic ingredients on your way, perhaps in Sarrians.

Gigondas

Afternoon

- Lunch: Drive up into the **Dentelles de Montmirail** for a picnic.
- Activity: Visit **Moulin de la Gardette** or **Clos de Caveau**.

Evening

- Dinner: There are lots of good options to eat in and around Gigondas. **L'Oustalet** is hard to beat and has one of the best Rhône wine lists in the world.

Sablet

Day 5, Thursday

Morning

- Activity: Take a drive around some of the prettier villages of the Vaucluse: Sablet, Séguret. Stop for a coffee in Vaison-la-Romaine.

Séguret

Afternoon

- Lunch: The cooking, service and wine list are all a cut above the average bistro at **Coteaux et Fourchettes**.
- Activity: Visit **Domaine Alary** in Cairanne or **Domaine des Coteaux des Travers** in Rasteau.

Evening

- Dinner: Arrive **Hôtel les Florets** a bit early, so you can have a drink on their spacious terrasse, the peaks of the Dentelles looming above. A delightful old-school French family-run hotel and restaurant, in the best way.

Vaison-la-Romaine

Day 6, Friday

Morning

Isle-sur-la-Sorgue

- Activity: Check out of the hotel. Drive to Isle-sur-la-Sorgue, take a walk through the town, check in to **La Maison sur la Sorgue**.

Afternoon

- Lunch: **Maison Moga** is one of the best delicatessens in the Vaucluse, with particularly good charcuterie, cheese and wine options. Get a sharing platter after you shop, or buy some goodies from here and **Maison Jouvaud** for a picnic and a paddle at **Le Partage des Eaux**.
- Activity: Visit **Château Unang** in Ventoux or **Domaine de Fontenille** in the Luberon.

Evening

- Dinner: **Le Vivier** has a terrace over the river and a very good wine list.

Day 7, Saturday

Morning

- Activity: Take a drive through the breathtaking scenery of the Luberon to the **Marché d'Apt** (see Markets pp86–88).

Afternoon

Bonnieux

- Lunch: Have lunch at **Le Moulin** and take a wander through the backstreets.
- Activity: Wander through the ancient ochre quarries of the Roussillon. Travel via Bonnieux if you can, a village perched on a mountaintop with incredible views.

Evening

- Dinner: **Restaurant Agastache** would make for a fitting end to your stay.

Day 8, Sunday

Check out, depart. Visit Isle-sur-la-Sorgue market if you have time!

Alternative two-day minibreak options during your Southern Rhône trip

The Ardèche – on the upper west bank of the Southern Rhône, the Ardèche river has cut deeply through the limestone bedrock to create dramatic gorges and cave systems – plenty to entertain lovers of the great outdoors.

Ardèche river

The Diois – wilder and less busy than the Ardèche river, the Drôme also offers aquatic adventures and great walking. The town of Die (pronounced 'dee') gives its name to the wine region of the Diois ('dee-wa'), and is one of many unspoilt towns and villages to explore.

Nîmes and the Camargue – though the wines and the terroir still have a Rhône accent, the Camargue feels like a different world to the rest of the Rhône Valley thanks to its estuarine landscape, unusual flora and fauna and local cuisine. The city of Nîmes was an important outpost of the Roman Empire, and there are still significant Roman remains here including a temple and amphitheatre – which is still used for bullfights. Beautiful gardens in the shape of Les Jardins de la Fontaine and several impressive museums add to its appeal.

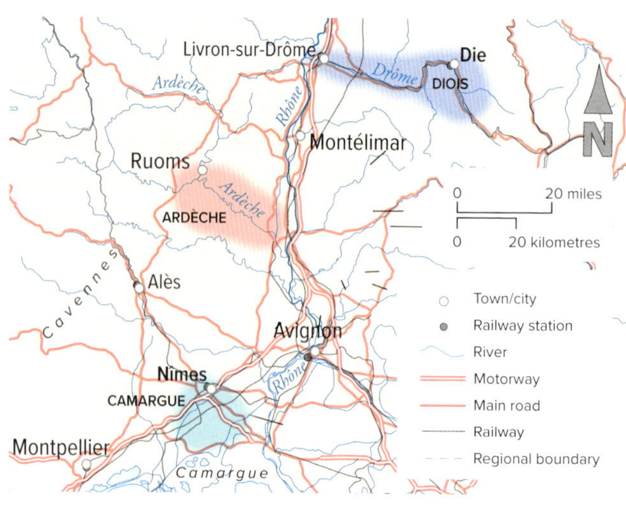

Things to do in Avignon

What is it about a walled city that piques our interest? Is it that those ancient ramparts suggest something precious within, and that we feel privileged to be admitted behind them?

Avignon

It's the obvious base for exploring the Southern Rhône. It's easy to get to thanks to the TGV station, and its central train station and bus garage opens up the immediate area if you don't have access to a car. Renting bicycles is another option: you can get to Châteauneuf-du-Pape in just over an hour by bike.

Renting a car gives you the most flexibility – Avignon is centrally placed for all the appellations of the Southern Rhône, and you can reach Tain l'Hermitage in the north in under two hours.

Being a walled city, Avignon is well-contained and explorable entirely on foot. There's plenty of choice of bars and restaurants – enough to keep you interested for a week or more – and here we also list the other attractions of this jewel of a city.

Le Palais des Papes

One of the largest medieval gothic buildings in Europe, the majestic Popes' Palace looms over Avignon. Construction started in 1252, and the building was used as the seat of the Papacy when it moved to Avignon from 1309 to 1376. It's open 9am to 7pm during high season; adults are €12, children €6.50. For this, you get to guide yourself around the building using a tablet that uses augmented reality to show how the place would have looked in the 14th century. It's well executed and really gives you an insight into how life would have been when the building was in use. You can visit the gardens too for a small supplement – it's worth it.
palais-des-papes.com

Rue Joseph Vernet

If you like shopping for clothes, you'll love Avignon. Start at the northern tip of Rue Joseph Vernet and make your way south – this is where most of the boutiques are found. As you work your way down, clothes shops are interspersed with interiors and other independent shops. A few side streets are worth exploring too: Rue de la Petite Fusterie,

Rue Saint-Agricol and, for menswear, Rue Falco de Baroncelli. There are even more small independent clothes shops dotted around Rue de la Bonneterie across the other side of town.

Shopping

There's a large pedestrianized shopping district to the southeast of the Place de l'Horloge, bordered by four roads: Rue de la République, Rue Carnot, Rue Grivolas and Rue des Lices. It's a rabbit warren of narrow streets lined with independent shops, selling everything imaginable: clothes, shoes, toys, chocolates, homewares, food, souvenirs… if you have gifts to buy, this is where to come. Even if you're not buying, it's a great place to people-watch and soak up the atmosphere – a paradise for the *flâneur*. A few stores worth marking on the map are La Carte à Jouer and L'Eau Vive for toys, Le Nid and Isabelle Erizé for homewares, objets d'art and gifts for grown-ups, Culinarion for kitchenware, Numéro 35 for local creators/artists and Mémoires for books.

Les Halles

Les Halles

You can find some of the finest products of Provence in the covered market of Les Halles. Even if you're not buying, it's a great place to greedily observe, smell the spices, sample some olives and marvel at the freshness of the fish and sheer variety of the goats cheeses. Of course, you'll find butchers, bakers and grocers, but also some gloriously ingredient-specific stands, such as the one that only sells various types of potato and onion. There are two little wine boutiques that are worth perusing too. Open every day except Monday, from 6am to 2pm.

avignon-leshalles.com

La Princière

La Princière on Place des Corps Saints is the best ice-cream shop in Avignon. They do have some seats both inside and out, but most people simply buy a cone (*un cornet*) or a little tub (*un pot*) to take away. Gariguette strawberry is a personal favourite, but whether you're into ice-cream or sorbet, classics or new creations, this place is not to be missed.
+33 (0)9 80 37 58 06

Collection Lambert

Yvon Lambert was a Parisian art dealer who built up a private collection of over 2,000 works of modern art and deposited 550 of them in Avignon. They are housed across two large 18th-century mansions on Rue Violette and include painting, sculpture, photography and installations from the 1960s to the early 21st century, with works from artists such as Cy Twombly, Jean-Michel Basquiat, Nan Goldin and Sol LeWitt. Entry is €12 for adults, €5 for young people and free for children under 12. If the restaurant is busy, Bèou Bistrot over the road is good.
collectionlambert.com

Le Pont d'Avignon

Le Pont d'Avignon

'Sur le pont d'Avignon,
l'on y danse, l'on y danse.
Sur le pont d'Avignon,
l'on y danse tous en rond.'

The original wooden bridge of the iconic Pont d'Avignon (or more correctly, the Pont Saint-Bénézet) was built in 1177, but destroyed during the Albigensian Crusade when Avignon was put to siege. It was rebuilt in stone in 1234, but since it was prone to collapse whenever the Rhône flooded, it was eventually abandoned in the mid-17th century. Only four arches remain, the bridge famously stopping in the middle of the river. Is it still a bridge if it doesn't reach the other side? A philosophical discussion best embarked upon late at night over a bottle of Châteauneuf.

Ile de la Barthelasse

To the north of Avignon, between two branches of the Rhône, is the largest river island in France – the 700ha Ile de la Barthelasse. Very few people live there because it's prone to flooding, so it's a great place to get away from the crowds. Take a walk along the towpath, or, even better, hire some bicycles and explore the island and enjoy the birdsong. Finish up at Vinotage, a wine bar on a barge, open 6.30pm to midnight from Wednesday to Saturday (also opens Mondays and Tuesdays during high season). See also Maison Manguin below.

Maison Manguin

Also on Ile de la Barthelasse is the Maison Manguin distillery. It was established in 1949 by Claude Manguin, son of fauviste painter Henri Manguin, who planted dozens of hectares of pear and peach trees on this fertile island. He distilled eaux-de-vie from the fruit; fruit spirits are still made here today using the artisanal method. There are various tour and tasting options available (from €5 to €15 per activity), but be sure to book in advance via the website. manguin.com

Villeneuve-lès-Avignon

Over the river from Ile de la Barthelasse is the village of Villeneuve-lès-Avignon, a 45-minute walk from Avignon. It's a picturesque, sleepy, photogenic neighbourhood which offers a pleasant contrast to the energy of Avignon. In fact, it feels like a mini-Avignon without so many tourists; like its larger sibling, it has a fortress built in the 14th century (in the shape of Font Saint-André, entry €7), and a handful of restaurants and independent shops.

Villeneuve-lès-Avignon

LISTINGS PREPARED BY

Matt Walls

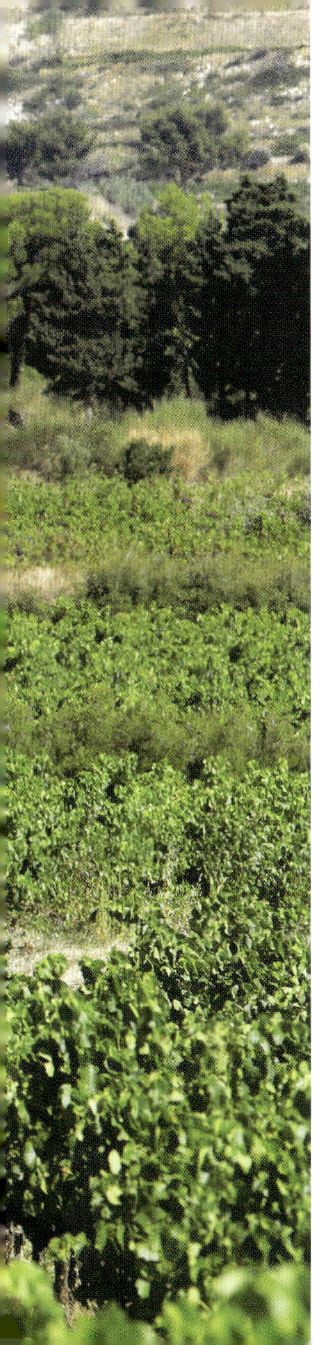

The Guide

Contents

Best producers to visit: tours and tastings

There are certain wine regions around the world that are closely associated with high-end, luxury wine tourism. The Rhône experience is altogether more authentic and down-to-earth. Rather than being served by sommeliers or met by cellar door staff, here you'll more likely be greeted by a member of the winemaker's family – or the winemaker. These are people who have lived there all their lives – you'll find them great sources of knowledge, not just of wine, but local cuisine, spots for a picnic, walking routes, wildlife...

Domaine de Beaurenard

Below are some suggestions that make excellent wines and offer an experience that's a cut above the average. But there are literally hundreds of wineries that will be happy to receive you throughout the Rhône Valley. If you're passing a property with a sign that says '*Degustation – vente*' (tasting and sales) – try your luck.

Entries in each section of The Guide are listed roughly north to south. Visiting details were correct at the time of publication but it's always worth contacting wineries in advance to ensure there are no unexpected changes to their routine.

Tips for visiting wineries

- It's always better to book in advance if you can. Sundays are usually sacrosanct, as are national holidays. Not all wineries are easy to find or have brilliant signage, so allow plenty of time to get there.
- Assume at least 90 minutes for a tour and tasting. If you have another appointment straight after, tell the winemaker early on so they can plan your visit accordingly.
- Unless stated, assume cellar doors and wineries will be closed to visitors around lunchtime.
- For those with limited mobility, working wineries can be difficult to navigate: uneven staircases, pipes across the floors, dark corridors... Take care while you're visiting.
- For children, wineries can be boring (and potentially dangerous) so remember to take some entertainment and keep them close to you at all times.
- If you're dropping in for a free tasting and you enjoyed the wines, then buy some! Try to carry some cash, as cards aren't always accepted.

Northern Rhône

Guigal, Ampuis

No family has had more impact on the wines of modern Côte-Rôtie than the Guigals. Today they are one of the biggest players in the Rhône Valley, with further properties in Châteauneuf-du-Pape and Tavel. Close to their headquarters in Ampuis is Le Caveau du Château, a grand, 19th-century home that has been beautifully renovated to receive visitors. Here they offer various themed tastings, including workshops around food and wine matching. You can also organize visits to their vineyards or cellar – both of which are spectacular. They also have a winemaking museum and a sizeable garden that

Guigal

children can explore while you sip a sample of La Turque in the sunshine. It's possible to drop in without an appointment, but for more in-depth guided tastings and visits it's better to reserve a place on lecaveauduchateau.com.

guigal.com

Domaine Niero, Condrieu

Rémi Niero is the third generation in his family to make wine in Condrieu, and today their estate is unquestionably one of the leading producers of this luxurious white wine. Two major projects are currently coming to fruition – in 2026, they should receive organic certification (a three-year process), and they are also due to open their new tasting room. Here, you'll be able to sample their wines (they also make Côte-Rôtie, Saint-Joseph and Crozes-Hermitage) and order some local snacks at the same time. It's in the old *office de tourisme* on the main road, and in keeping with the spirit of the old building, they'll be happy to point you in the direction of the best places to eat, stay and explore in the village and further afield. To book in advance, call +33 (0)4 74 56 86 99 or email contact@vins-niero.com.

vins-niero.com

Where winemakers dine

At Maison M Chapoutier in Tain l'Hermitage, the staff always stop at lunchtime to eat. We have a chef-led dining table, providing a friendly setting for our employees and guests. I often eat there, but sometimes I cross the street to **Marius Bistro**, located in our hotel opposite the winery. Our current chef, ranked third in the world championship of *pâté en croûte*, offers bistronomic cuisine combining Provençal and Lyon traditions. For a gastronomic experience, I enjoy **La Pyramide** by Patrick Henriroux in Vienne, where you can enjoy traditional cuisine, based on harmony between dishes and wines. In Valence, for those looking for culinary innovation, **Anne-Sophie Pic** offers ever-evolving, original creations.

Michel Chapoutier, Maison M Chapoutier, Tain L'Hermitage

Domaine Laurent Fayolle, Gervans

The village of Gervans, north of Hermitage, is surrounded by a small enclave of granite that makes for particularly elegant wines. Domaine Laurent Fayolle is one of the several excellent estates to be found here, and he makes some of the best wines in Crozes-Hermitage. He produces several different whites and reds, starting with the entry-level Sens, to Les Pontaix (made of 40-year-old vines) up to his Clos les Cornirets (from 60-year-old vines). He also bottles small quantities of red and white Hermitage too, and a very fine Saint-Péray. Winery visits and tastings are welcome, but must be booked in advance on +33 (0)4 75 03 33 74; the price varies depending on the wines tasted, but it's typically between €15 to €20 per person.

fayolle-filsetfille.fr

Chapoutier, Tain l'Hermitage

Even before Tain l'Hermitage saw many tourists, Chapoutier – famous for the quality of its Hermitage wines – had a permanent cellar door open to visitors. It's always busy, and is now open every day of the week – even on Sundays. As wine tourism has warmed up in this part of the Rhône, so has Chapoutier's offering. Today, they have a hotel called Fac et Spera (see Best hotels in the Rhône Valley p132) that includes a wine bar and restaurant, not to mention a small gîte, La Tour du Pavillon in the vineyards of Hermitage itself (see Best

Chapoutier

Delas

vineyard stays and other accommodation p142). You can book tastings at the boutique across different themes, ranging from €39 per person up to €130 per person for their top vineyards. They even hire out e-bikes.

chapoutier.com

Delas, Tain l'Hermitage

The large merchant house of Delas was somewhat in the doldrums before being bought by the Champagne Louis Roederer group in 1997. Since then, every part of the business has been bolstered to reclaim its place in the Rhône premier league. A major part of this was constructing a new winery in the heart of Tain l'Hermitage, which is among the most architecturally impressive in the region. You can see for yourself with a tour of their new facility, along with a tasting of their wines. There are various options, depending on the wines you want to try, ranging from €40 to €65 per person. There is no on-site restaurant, but resident chefs can organize a personalized lunch if desired (needs to be booked in advance). To arrange a visit, email contact@delas.com.

delas.com

Domaine Alain Voge, Cornas

Let's be honest; the village of Cornas doesn't thrum with attractions. It doesn't even have a restaurant (though there is a bakery if you need a snack). But from the main street you can see the legendary hillside that rises abruptly beyond the houses, which gives birth to some of the most captivating and powerful reds in the Northern Rhône.

Park in the main car park and make your way to Domaine Alain Voge to taste some great examples. Alain was a pioneering winemaker before he passed away, and the winery and barrel rooms are still underneath the family home. They're also celebrated for the quality of their white Saint-Péray. Visits can be organized by email: contact@alain-voge.com.

alain-voge.com

Domaine Rémy Nodin, Saint-Péray

Easily located in the pretty village of Saint-Péray, Rémy Nodin is a passionate young winemaker who knows the region inside out. Along with still wines, he also makes delicious sparkling Saint-Péray – once prized, but now almost forgotten. You can pop in for a tasting of their wines for a modest fee on Fridays and Saturdays. Even better, add a tour of their winery or vineyards with a series of matching dishes to enjoy alongside. To book in advance, call +33 (0)4 75 40 35 90. There are good options nearby for lunch or dinner (Auberge de Crussol, Aux Coeurs Fidèles) and an independent wine shop (Les Crus d'Sol). A day in Saint-Péray can be an appealing option.

remy-nodin.fr

Southern Rhône

Domaine Peylong, Suze

The Drôme Valley makes a refreshing contrast to the rest of the Rhône Valley – dramatic, green and mountainous. They do things a little differently here – most of their output is sparkling, and they grow lots of varieties that aren't found elsewhere in the region. At under 4ha, the organic Domaine Peylong might be a small estate but they grow 13 different varieties and make some intriguingly original wines that offer extraordinary value for money. The cellar door and garden are open every day from Monday to Saturday, 5pm to 7pm for a free tasting. If you book in advance, they also offer guided tours around the vineyards, pizza and pétanque, or larger meals made from local products – see their website for details or call +33 (0)6 02 50 83 64.

peylong.com

Domaine Saladin, Saint-Marcel-d'Ardèche

The Saladin family have farmed in the village of Saint-Marcel-d'Ardèche for 21 generations, and they have always worked organically. If you find yourself in this corner of the Southern Rhône, it's the perfect place to stock up. The estate is currently in the hands of friendly sisters Elisabeth and Marie-Laurence, who make Natural wines of great charm, precision and drinkability. The cellar door is open Monday to Friday; on weekends it's advisable to call in advance on +33 (0)4 75 04 63 20.

domaine-saladin.com

Domaine Peylong

Domaine des Escaravailles

Domaine Vallot, Vinsobres

Vinsobres feels a little wilder and more wooded than some of the better-known Rhône appellations. There are lots of estates worth visiting, however, such as the biodynamic Domaine Vallot, which has been working according to the phases of the moon since 2007. The estate is now in the hands of Anaïs Vallot, and her wines have great intensity and verve. She offers free tastings from Monday to Saturday; even better, book in advance to order a platter of local goat cheeses, olives and dark chocolate to accompany your wines. Winery tours are available for groups. To book, call Anaïs on +33 (0)4 75 26 03 24 or email her at anais@domainevallot.com.

domainevallot.com

Domaine des Escaravailles, Rasteau

Escaravay is the word for beetle in the local dialect. It's the nickname that the inhabitants of Rasteau used to use for the Black Penitents, monks of Avignon that owned this estate in the 17th century. The Ferran family purchased it in 1964, and it's now in the hands of third-generation Madeline Ferran, who makes brilliant Rasteau of serious depth and concentration. You can drop in to their cellar door at the estate for a free tasting; it's open all year round, Monday to Saturday. They also have a boutique in Vaison-la-Romaine called Jas Laurine, which is open from Tuesday to Saturday, May to September. In summer 2026, they plan to open a 2km path around their estate with views across the valley – feel free to take a picnic!

domaine-escaravailles.com

Moulin de la Gardette, Gigondas

The name Gigondas is thought to come from the Latin word 'jocunditas', meaning great pleasure or enjoyment – which is exactly what the village has in store for you. It's partly thanks to the beauty of the settlement and its surrounding countryside, and also thanks to the quality of the wines – and those of biodynamic Moulin de la Gardette are among the very best. Jean-Baptiste Meunier has recently been joined by his daughter Zoë and together they make three different Gigondas cuvées from their 25 plots of vines, all of which are delicious. They have a lightness of touch and spellbinding perfume that make for a particularly distinctive style. The Meuniers have a boutique in the Gigondas village square which is open for tasting and sales (closed Sundays); visits to the vineyard can be organized with advance notice by contacting moulingardette@wanadoo.fr.

moulindelagardette.com

Where winemakers dine

One of my favourite restaurants is **Le Tournesol**, known for its creative gourmet cuisine. They have delicious tapas made from locally sourced ingredients, and pair them with an excellent selection of wines. It's a very welcoming and pleasant place, and the journey to get there from Maison Delas is truly scenic, crossing the Rhône river with breathtaking views of the Hermitage and Saint-Joseph vineyards. Along the way, you'll also pass by **Le Chaudron**, a historic restaurant really worth recommending. It focuses on showcasing regional products and talented winemakers, offering exquisite dishes complemented by carefully curated wine pairings you won't forget.

Jacques Grange, technical director and chief winemaker, Delas Frères, Tain L'Hermitage

Domaine la Monardière, Vacqueyras

Not many Rhône Crus make wines in all three colours; it's even more unusual to find an estate that excels at all three. Domaine la Monardière is one of them. Damien Vache took over the family estate in 2007, the same year that they gained organic certification. He now makes wines of wonderful freshness and vitality from 15 different varieties. Their bright cellar door is open from Monday to Friday from November to March, then Monday to Saturday from April to September. They don't charge for informal tastings for groups of fewer than six people. For a more in-depth tasting of five wines and a tour of the winery, you need to book in advance at info@monardiere.fr or call +33 (0)4 90 65 87 20.

monardiere.fr

Domaine Le Sang des Cailloux, Sarrians

Le Sang des Cailloux ('the blood of the stones') was established in 1975, and in the 1980s Serge Férigoule joined as a vineyard worker. He ended up buying the estate in 1990, and promptly converted it to organic farming. He quickly gained a reputation for the freshness and finesse of his wines. His son Frédéri now runs the show, and has since gained them biodynamic certification. Neither father nor son is afraid to express his opinion; their reds and whites are now among the most pure and elegant in the Southern Rhône, and still offer good value for money. A visit here is a must if you're passing through Vacqueyras. Book via the website (closed weekends).

sangdescailloux.com

Château Pesquié, Mormoiron

Those intrepid enough to explore Mont Ventoux and its surrounds will be richly rewarded – rugged, unspoilt terrain, fabulous views and some excellent wines that offer surprising value for money. One of the first private estates to set up here was Château Pesquié, established by the Chaudière family in 1990. Now run by brothers Alex and Frédéric, the 100ha estate offers a host of activities. Drop in for a free tasting without a reservation any day of the week (closed on Sundays between October and Easter). They also offer self-guided walks around the estate with audio and video snippets from the owners (€5); order in advance and you can add a generous picnic for €25 per person. Or go for the full guided tour with extended tasting for

Domaine Le Sang des Cailloux

€20 per person. They put on various events throughout the year: concerts, truffle dinners, their famous White Party in July… For enquiries, email reception@chateaupesquie.com; you can book via their website.

chateaupesquie.com

Domaine de Cristia, Courthézon

The Châteauneufs of Domaine de Cristia often come out at the top of blind tastings thanks to their combination of power and finesse. Owner Baptiste Grangeon owns vineyards across a range of other appellations that makes for an interesting comparison – and don't miss his two 'Chapelle Saint Théodoric' Châteauneufs that are fast gaining cult status. Drop in for a tasting (€8 per person, deductible against a purchase), or book a more in-depth visit with optional snacks or picnic from €29 to €75. They also have a modern guest house with five independent rooms to rent in the vines near Courthézon, and can offer homemade breakfasts and packed lunches on request. To book or enquire, call +33 (0)4 90 70 24 09, or email contact@cristia.com for tastings, reservation@cristia.com for rooms.

cristia.com

Domaine de Beaurenard, Châteauneuf-du-Pape

Châteauneuf-du-Pape is a big name in the world of wine, but many of its estates aren't geared up to receive tourists. Domaine de Beaurenard, however, is happy to have visitors all year round – which is particularly good news given that its wines are among the best in the appellation. The Coulon family are a friendly and welcoming bunch, and you can learn a lot here – they use all 18 permitted grape varieties, farm biodynamically and are happy to explain its more esoteric aspects, like burying cow horns filled with dung. They are also adept at making rare white Châteauneuf. The tasting room is open during the week with or without a booking. During the weekend, they don't even close for lunch. Visits to the cellars and the winemaking museum are available on request, but must be booked via the website.

beaurenard.fr

Château la Nerthe, Châteauneuf-du-Pape

If you don't have long to explore Châteauneuf-du-Pape, then a visit to Château la Nerthe is a good option. With roots going

Domaine de Beaurenard

Domaine de la Mordorée

back to 1560, it's one of the oldest and most historically important wine estates in the country. With its large mansion house in wooded parkland, it's also one of the most picturesque estates in Châteauneuf. Crucially, though, the wines are excellent – they have 100ha of excellent holdings in some very desirable parts of the appellation. Unusually, their whites are just as good as their reds. Informal tastings are available in the estate shop without an appointment seven days a week from May to September; closed on Sundays outside this period. More in-depth tastings and visits are recommended, however, ranging from €25 to €100 per person. To book, call +33 (0)4 90 83 59 04 or email visit@chateaulanerthe.fr.

chateaulanerthe.fr

Domaine de la Mordorée, Tavel

Founded in 1986, Domaine de la Mordorée has rapidly established itself as a leading player in Tavel, Lirac and Châteauneuf-du-Pape thanks to its powerful, expressive and vibrant wines. Based in the village of Tavel, the estate is now managed by third generation Ambre Delorme, who has recently converted the estate to biodynamic. Free tasting at their cellar door, no appointment necessary. Open Monday to Friday, Saturdays during high season, closed Sundays. Private tastings in their tasting room and vineyards tours are available by appointment. To book, call +33 (0)4 66 50 00 75 or email info@domaine-mordoree.com.

domaine-mordoree.com

Château la Verrerie, Puget

If you're visiting the Southern Rhône, it's well worth dipping a toe in the Luberon – you could stay for a week and not get bored in this achingly picturesque part of France. Puget is an easy drive that's less than an hour from Avignon, and is surrounded by pretty villages. It's also home to Château la Verrerie, one of the first private estates to be established in the Luberon, in 1981. They make bold, sun-drenched wines and offer various wine-related activities on their 56ha organic domaine. There are various types of tours and tastings available, and you can also order a well-stocked Provençal picnic basket for your visit. To book, call +33 (0)4 90 08 97 97 or email boutique@chateau-la-verrerie.fr.

chateau-la-verrerie.com

Château la Verrerie

Château de Nages

Château de Nages, Caissargues

The area around Nîmes and the Camargue, the coastal Regional Nature Park just south of Arles, makes for a great day trip while you're exploring the Southern Rhône – it has a unique, dreamy coastal vibe. Drop into Château de Nages, a leading proponent of regenerative agriculture. They have a 2km self-guided trail around the property that explains their philosophy and practice. Other free activities include tastings, visiting the aromatic garden and various games for young children. They also offer VIP tastings by reservation on a variety of themes: blind tastings, an introduction to Rhône Valley grape varieties, vertical tastings, blending workshops and more. Each includes food pairings and ranges from €20 to €40 per person. For info on the events throughout the year, visit the website. For groups and private tastings, book in advance at info@chateaudenages.com or by phone at +33 (0)4 66 38 44 33.

famillegassier.fr

Best hotels in the Rhône Valley

When it comes to hotels in Lyon, you're spoilt for choice. Among the vineyards of the Northern Rhône, however, there aren't so many – it's only recently started attracting international travellers in significant numbers. There are some luxurious options topping and tailing the region in Vienne and Valence, and several dependable places around Ampuis and Tain l'Hermitage.

InterContinental Lyon - Hotel Dieu

There is an abundance of choice throughout the south, with countless hotels dotted all over the region – whether you're looking for clean lines and modern facilities, or you prefer to bathe in the faded grandeur that Provence does so well. Most of the larger hotels are in and around Avignon, but there's no need to base yourself in a city; if you'd prefer to stay in a village – or even in the middle of nowhere – you'll find somewhere that caters for you.

Northern Rhône

Villa Maïa, Lyon

€€€€€

Considering that Villa Maïa only opened its doors in 2017, it feels remarkably well-established. It's partly thanks to its Art Deco-inspired décor, created by celebrated interior designer Jacques Grange, which gives this elegant address a contemporary but timeless feel. It's located in a quiet neighbourhood on the Fourvière hill, with views across the city, which offers the best of both worlds – you are far from the crowds, but can reach Place Bellecour in less than 20 minutes on foot; to get back up, you can take the funicular railway. There are 34 rooms and suites in total, giving the place an intimate feel, with large indoor baths, a spa and a small, wild, grassy garden. The compact bar offers non-stop service all day, and is open to all – not just hotel guests. There is no on-site restaurant, but next door you'll find Christian Têtedoie's Michelin-starred restaurant and bistro. It's a hotel with an undeniable cool factor.

villa-maia.com

InterContinental Lyon - Hotel Dieu, Lyon

€€€€

The Grand Hôtel Dieu, on the right bank of the Rhône, spent most of its 900-year life as a hospital, but that chapter came to an end in 2010. Its rooms, halls and cloisters are now inhabited by a high-end retail centre and the InterContinental Lyon - Hotel Dieu. The 144-room hotel opened its doors in 2019, and still feels box fresh. It's suitable for both business travellers and couples on holiday; it's a professional, smart, luxurious establishment that speaks the international language of fine hotels. Thanks to its long façade, half the elegant, high-ceilinged rooms have views over the Rhône. There are two dining options: their restaurant Epona and bar Le Dôme. The wine list they

InterContinental Lyon – Hotel Dieu

share isn't exactly cheap but there are plenty of good wines to choose from surrounding wine regions and even from outside France. Le Dôme deserves a special mention – it's a jaw-dropping space that used to be a chapel for patients. Today they offer a short food menu, wines by the glass and even wine and mixology workshops.

lyon.intercontinental.com

Domaine de Clairefontaine, Chonas-l'Amballan

€€€

One of the best hotel options near to Ampuis is Domaine de Clairefontaine, a 17th-century manor house in 3ha of grounds just across the river in the tiny village of Chonas-l'Amballan. You can either stay in the grand old house itself, or in the residence just across the large lawn, which has larger rooms but in a more modern building. Either way, you'll get to enjoy the tranquil setting and (glass of Condrieu in hand) watch the swans glide over the pond. The older building also houses a Michelin-starred restaurant where Philippe Girardon, awarded Meilleur Ouvrier de France in 1997, produces elegant dishes from hyper-local produce. Sommelier Dominique Viala has been looking after the wine collection since 1992, and it's a

Where winemakers dine

On the road between Die and Châtillon, the **Restaurant ABC** is run by the passionate young chef Anthony Bonnard. His 'gastronomically local' cuisine evolves with the seasons and the region's produce. The understated and authentic atmosphere reflects a true passion for surprising pairings and combinations. Whether for business or family lunches, I love this restaurant.

Fabien Lombard, Domaine Peylong, Suze (Diois)

strong list with plenty of choice. Part of the hotel is Le Cottage, a more modern building 10 minutes' walk away, which offers affordable contemporary rooms and is home to a good bistro, with a concise but well-thought-out wine list. As you drive back towards Ampuis, the views of Côte-Rôtie are breathtaking.

domaine-de-clairefontaine.fr

Fac et Spera, Tain l'Hermitage

€€€

Fac et spera ('Do and Hope') is the motto of the Chapoutier family, which owns this hotel. It's on the same road as the Chapoutier boutique, and you can see the hill of Hermitage itself from the hotel pool. It's bigger and has more facilities than most accommodation options in the Northern Rhône: secure car park, small spa and separate bar and restaurant. For those that like to pair Hermitage with steak, they also have a dry-ageing cabinet stocked with various cuts and origins of beef. With Tournon just a walk away, Fac et Spera offers a convenient base from which to explore this part of the Northern Rhône.

facetspera.fr

Fac et Spera

Hôtel de la Villeon, Tournon

€€€€

Tucked away in the sleepy backstreets of Tournon, Hôtel de la Villeon is undoubtedly one of the finest places to stay in the Northern Rhône. Damien and Delphine Segond converted this characterful 18th-century mansion house into a 16-room hotel and opened the doors in 2015. Rooms and suites vary in size and are tastefully decorated to a very high standard. Behind the house itself is a shady, terraced network of gardens where you can drink a cool glass of white Saint-Joseph before walking to whichever local restaurant takes your fancy. There's also a new swimming pool and gym with panoramic views across the river to the hill of Hermitage. Their small but stylish bar is open to all.

hoteldelavilleon.com

Hôtel Pic, Valence

€€€€€

Anne-Sophie Pic is one of France's most fêted chefs. Her three-star restaurant in Valence (see Best fine dining in the Rhône p152) is famous throughout France and beyond, but what is less well-known is her hotel, which is located at the same address: 16 rooms and suites that opened in 1997. Fashioning hotel rooms that are in keeping with the exquisite dining room downstairs is a challenge to which they have successfully risen; the accommodation here does not disappoint. The luminous rooms come in shades of white and silver, with silk, leather and rosewood adding the fine detail. Guests can make use of the restaurant bar, lounge and exotic garden, and they have exclusive use of the swimming pool. Though it's not a prerequisite to eat in the restaurant downstairs, most guests can't resist. An unforgettable pitstop between the Northern Rhône and the south.

anne-sophie-pic.com

Hôtel Pic

Southern Rhône

Villa Sainte-Anne, Gigondas

€€€

A new and welcome addition to the Gigondas environs, Villa Sainte-Anne is a contemporary guest house with five rooms that offers elegant, spacious bedrooms and chic shared spaces, both inside and out. It doesn't offer a full service like a hotel, which is ideal if you prefer to be semi-autonomous – the reception is manned in the morning and afternoon, but apart from that, you can get on with things yourself and make use of the kitchen and dining area. There's a car park available, but the village itself is just a 10-minute walk, with all its eating and drinking options. The villa is owned by the Amadieu family, which has been making wine in the village since 1929, so you're in good hands if you need any advice. Don't miss the breakfast.

oenotourisme.pierre-amadieu.com

Hôtel Crillon le Brave, Crillon le Brave

€€€€€

The Hôtel Crillon le Brave is one of the wonders of Provence. It's not a single building but occupies a whole segment of the village, knitting together nine 17th- and 18th-century houses to create a single entity, comprising 34 rooms and suites. It's located between Mont Ventoux and the Dentelles de Montmirail, which gives the place a sense of tranquillity and privacy – and the views from the terrace are breathtaking.

Villa Sainte-Anne

La Mère Germaine

You can eat very well at their restaurant, La Table du Ventoux, and the spa area reflects the same level of Provençal luxury you'll find throughout. If you're looking for indulgence among the vineyards, this is where to go.

crillonlebrave.com

La Mère Germaine, Châteauneuf-du-Pape

€€€

Germaine Vion was a chef in the French president's office until 1922, when she bought the Hôtel Bellevue in Châteauneuf-du-Pape. Its reputation grew, and eventually it took the name of its *patronne*. By the 2000s, however, it was a shadow of its former self. In 2019, it was purchased by Isabelle and Arnaud Strasser, who completely renovated the building and redecorated its rooms. They have done an outstanding job, and today La Mère Germaine can once again be considered among the finest hotels in the region. Since buying and renovating an additional neighbouring guesthouse, they now have 12 rooms which are equipped to a high standard, and you'll have access to secure parking, a neat spa, not to mention their Michelin-starred restaurant (see Best fine dining in the Rhône p152). If you're travelling with family or friends and are looking for something larger or more private, in 2024 they opened two private houses in the village that you can hire in their entirety, one sleeping ight with pool and garden, another sleeping six.

lameregermaine.com

Where winemakers dine

Among my favourite restaurants, **La Cuisine du Marché** in Nyons holds a very special place. Florian and Valentin, two food and wine enthusiasts, offer precise, elaborate and flavourful cuisine. The flavour combinations are perfectly balanced, and the extensive wine list will delight every palate. In Roaix, **La Belle Etoile** is another favourite, just a stone's throw from our estate. This place offers authentic, local cuisine with a surprising touch of originality. The welcome is warm, and in summer, the terrace is enchanting. These two restaurants share a love of quality produce, attention to detail and the desire to provide their customers with a memorable experience. They're unmissable in my opinion.

Madeline Ferran, Domaine des Escaravailles, Rasteau

Le Colombier, Venasque

€

Perched on a cliff, Venasque is one of the oldest and most beautiful villages in the Southern Rhône, and one with a rich history – it was briefly the capital of the Comtat Venaissin, a sizeable chunk of the Vaucluse that was owned by the Pope from 1274 to 1791. Le Colombier was recently taken over by a young couple with plenty of hotel experience and it offers a convenient spot from which to explore Ventoux. Rooms are small and simply decorated, but the package as a whole is pleasant, and the prices affordable. With an ample swimming pool, pétanque pitch and hotel bar, it's ideal for young families, and just a short walk into the centre of the village.

lecolombier-venasque.com

La Mirande, Avignon

€€€€€

On a quiet backstreet just behind the Palais des Papes in Avignon is the five-star La Mirande. The building is a feast for the senses; it brims with fine fabrics and *objets d'art* and the walls echo with 700 years of good living. It now has 26 bedrooms, all decorated with exquisite French fabrics. There are multiple dining and drinking options here (see Best fine dining in the Rhône p152), and their Michelin-starred gastronomic restaurant serves some of the most refined dishes in Avignon. You can breakfast in the beautiful garden – a rare treat within the city walls. If you're looking for luxury in Avignon, La Mirande is the obvious choice.

la-mirande.fr

Hôtel d'Europe, Avignon

€€€€

After a day visiting vineyards under the summer sun, the cool courtyard of the Hôtel d'Europe feels like a sanctuary: jasmine-scented, under the shade of an immense plane tree. This venerable 44-room 16th-century hotel feels like it has seen it all, and offers comfortable, old-fashioned luxury. It's located in one of Avignon's smaller squares that's lined with bars and restaurants. It can be lively in the evenings; if you're a light sleeper, request a room towards the back of the building. Its restaurant La Vieille Fontaine isn't exactly at the forefront of contemporary décor or cuisine, but you can find some real gems on the wine list.

heurope.com

La Mirande

Best vineyard stays and other accommodation

Hotels are just one option when it comes to accommodation – there are plenty of other choices, including guesthouses, gîtes, campsites... even treehouses. Or why not stay at a winery? Many estates – and even some ancient châteaux – have cottages or converted barns in the grounds.

Cabanes Perchées

Northern Rhône

Huttopia, various sites

€€

Huttopia was established in 1999 with a single campsite in southeast France. Today, there are 152 sites across three continents. Most of them are in France, and there are five within the Rhône Valley. Most have a mix of pitches for tents and motor homes, and semi-permanent, wood-and-canvas accommodation of various types and sizes. Either way, you'll find a swimming pool, restaurant, bar and a packed timetable of daily activities for children and adults alike. Even their most basic 'prêt à camper' accommodation has a real bed, a fridge, grill, table, chairs and a wooden terrace. More luxurious cabins have running water, toilets, showers... others have wood-burning stoves. There are several elements that make Huttopia a cut above most traditional campsites: the cleanliness and good order of the sites; the professionalism and warmth of the staff; the natural beauty of the settings. So you feel like you're getting back to nature, but it still feels like a holiday rather than a test of survival skills. Most sites purposely don't offer a Wi-Fi connection (there is a connected terminal at reception should you really need it).

Pays de Condrieu – the most recently opened site at the time of writing, so everything feels brand new. It's situated on the plateau above the village, with beautiful views. And just a short drive from Condrieu and Côte-Rôtie, and not far from Lyon.

Sud Ardèche – a 14ha site close to Vallon Pont d'Arc, perfect for exploring the Gorges de l'Ardèche. There are Nordic hot tubs in a little outdoor spa area to soothe your aching muscles when you get back.

Le Moulin – a smaller 7ha site with direct access to the Ardèche river for swimming. It's located in Saint-Martin-d'Ardèche, a 10-minute drive from both Domaine Saladin and Domaine de Couron – both of which are well worth visiting.

Dieulefit – 20km north is the Diois; 20km south is Visan and Valréas – so there are many wine villages nearby to explore... but with hot tubs, saunas and wild swimming in the lake there's plenty to do on-site as well.

Fontvieille – situated in a pine forest in the Alpilles Regional Park, it feels far from civilization – but it's just a 15-minute walk from the village of Fontvieille, with its shops, restaurants and excellent wine shops.

huttopia.com

Clos de la Garelle, Crozes

€€€€

Clos de la Garelle is a renovated villa deep in the countryside near the village of Crozes, a short drive from Tain l'Hermitage. It's owned by Damien and Delphine Segond of Hotel de la Villeon (see p136), and you can expect a similar quality of interior, this time with a touch of chinoiserie thanks to the history of this former hunting lodge. The six double bedrooms are simpler than those at the hotel in Tournon, but most of your time will no doubt be spent in the common areas – the house is rented out as a single unit. It has a large outdoor pool a few minutes from the house, a family kitchen (and separate prep kitchen), a hammam and a separate one-bed flat. The perfect place to celebrate your next big birthday.

hoteldelavilleon.com

Clos de la Garelle

La Tour du Pavillon

La Tour du Pavillon, Tain l'Hermitage

€€

There are very few private houses on the hill of Hermitage itself, and certainly no hotels. But if you look closely, you'll see a little white two-storey building among the vines. It belongs to Chapoutier – and you can stay there. La Tour du Pavillon sleeps two people, and you can make use of the small kitchen and dining area within. Imagine sitting among the vines, drinking a bottle of Hermitage on the hill itself, the orange sun slowly dipping. You can also hire electric bikes to explore the area, and there are various tasting experiences in the boutique a short walk away.

chapoutier-gites.com

La Péniche B&B, Tournon

€€

There's something magical about waking up to see sunlight, reflected from the river, dancing on the ceiling. When you get out of bed, the Rhône is nearly at eye level. La Péniche is an atypical and fun place to stay for a number of reasons. Firstly – well, it's a boat. Secondly, there are no staff on hand – you're sent a QR code that unlocks the shared, glass-walled upper deck and your bedroom downstairs. The rooms, though lacking certain amenities like fridges, all have air conditioning and are decorated to a higher standard than you might expect. There is a shared kitchen area upstairs but you'll have to pop to the shops to buy anything to eat

La Péniche

or drink – it's moored close to the main square (and car park), so you don't have far to walk. Breakfast, however, can be provided – as can secure bicycle storage, which is handy as La Péniche is on the ViaRhôna cycle route.

lapeniche.biz

Camping Ferme Le Simondon, Plats

€

Take the twisting road up from Mauves towards the village of Plats and eventually you'll reach Simondon Farm. It's cool and airy up here, and the views are tremendous. Whether you're staying in one of the ancient, thick-walled cottages or on the campsite, you can make use of the heated outdoor pool and restaurant, and commune with the various chickens, sheep and donkeys that live on-site.

restaurant-gite-camping-simondon.fr

Cabanes Perchées du Safari de Peaugres, Peaugres

€€€€

If you like the idea of getting up close and personal with wild animals, spend a day at the 80-hectare Safari de Peaugres, near Annonay. There are 1,300 animals from over 120 species, many of which roam right past you in enclosures you can enter. You can't touch the monkeys, but there is a petting zoo. Even better, you can stay the night in one of 20 raised wooden cabins right above the bear and wolf compound. The cabins are big, solidly made, with kitchens and eating areas and plenty of playful touches. They come in a variety of shapes and sizes – one even has an extra two-bed UFO on its terrace with a view of the stars. The biggest sleeps 12; there are also some two-bed floor-level cabins with windows over the cheetah compound. On Fridays during the summer, they invite local winemakers to pour their wines in the grounds for guests. If you want to stay on Saturday nights or during school holidays, book well in advance.

lesnuits.safari-peaugres.com

Southern Rhône

Notre Dame de Cousignac, Bourg-Saint-Andéol

€

If you're considering staying in the southern Ardèche, there are a number of reasons that make Notre Dame de Cousignac a smart choice. This working wine estate has been in the Pommier family for seven generations; the wines, certified organic, come highly recommended. On the property there are five guestrooms and a separate two-storey gîte with original stone walls and a jacuzzi. All the accommodation shares another hot tub and a pool, and there's

Cabanes Perchées du Safari de Peaugres

Where winemakers dine

As an upcoming area, a great gastronomic scene is developing in the Ventoux. I recommend the wonderful bistro food and stellar wine list of **Vin Ensen** in Caromb, presented with a warm welcome by sommeliers Hugo and Jean-Philippe. Then there is **Chez Serge**, an institution for wine and truffles in Carpentras. **La Calade** in Blauvac is a remarkable and creative restaurant with a beautiful view of the valley, run by young chef Janis and his partner Margaux.

Frédéric Chaudière, Château Pesquié, Mormoiron (Ventoux)

an on-site organic restaurant. They offer a range of activities: a wine tasting with charismatic owner Raphaël; a visit to the 6th-century chapel; vineyard tours on electric bikes; not to mention massage, yoga and tai-chi. Other reliable wineries such as Domaine Bonetto-Fabrol and Domaine de Grangeneuve are a short drive away.

domainedecousignac.fr

Camping Les Rives de l'Aygues, Tulette

€

This tranquil campsite near the village of Tulette is on a 3.5ha site with nearly 100 spacious pitches. 'Les Rives de l'Aygues' means 'the banks of the Aygues' – the shallow Aygues river is just a short walk away, offering endless entertainment for small children, and picturesque walking. There's a pool in the campsite itself, three play areas and a snack bar. There is a range of accommodation options, including mobile homes, chalets and permanent wood-and-canvas structures. The environmental commitments here – installing bird boxes and insect hotels, avoiding pesticides – add to the feeling that you're surrounded by nature. You're also encircled by some of the best Côtes-du-Rhône Villages.

lesrivesdelaygues.com

Domaine de la Verrière, Crestet

€€€

Lovers of Rhône wines might have come across the stylish Chêne Bleu wines; Domaine de la Verrière, situated in a UNESCO nature reserve in the Dentelles de Montmirail near Crestet, is where they are made. People have lived in this secluded spot for over 1,000 years, but when it was bought by Xavier and Nicole Rolet in 1993 it was in ruins. The renovation took nearly 12 years, and when you visit you see why it took so long – everything has been done with meticulous attention to detail, with sustainability at heart. There are many reasons to come here – to visit the winery, to eat or even to enrol on the Extreme Wine course, hosted by Masters of Wine. There are seven rooms and suites, all in keeping with the medieval Provençal chic of the estate. It can sleep 17 in total if you hire the whole estate. You won't want to leave. A word of advice if you're visiting: set your satnav to the village of Crestet first, then navigate to La Verrière from there.

Domaine de la Verrière

chenebleu.com/stay

Mas de l'Evajade, Beaumes de Venise

€

If you're looking for somewhere a bit different to lay your head, how about sleeping in a huge barrel in a vineyard? Mas de l'Evajade in Beaumes de Venise has just such a thing, with a double bed, an optional single, a kitchen, shower, eating area, air con... everything you need for a comfortable stay. There are four additional simple gîtes with access to a shared open kitchen and small pool, and a large modern apartment that sleeps eight. The friendly owners are also vine growers, and will make you feel very welcome. With swings, toys and a garden to explore it's ideal for families with young children.

evajade.fr

Domaine Saint-Préfert, Châteauneuf-du-Pape

€€

Isabel Ferrando doesn't come from a long line of winemakers,

Domaine Saint-Préfert

but she still felt the call of the vines. In 2002 she noticed that an old winery was up for sale, and, with the birth of her daughter Guillemette, she decided to take the plunge. Isabel's wines have been among the best in Châteauneuf-du-Pape for many years, and she has recently renovated two gîtes on the property, one that sleeps four, another that sleeps six. There's a good-sized swimming pool with views of the vineyards, and you can expect to spot plenty of birds and butterflies – the estate has been certified biodynamic since 2019. For more information call +33 (0)4 90 83 75 03 or email contact@familleferrando.com.

familleferrando.com

Mas de l'Evajade

Metafort, Méthamis

€€

At the apex of the hilltop town of Méthamis there's a tall building: an old fortress with a long history. It was bought in 2019 by Elsa and Arnaud who transformed it into a striking B&B that feels like a slice of rural Ibiza in the Vaucluse. The aromatic garden and swimming pool have views that plunge down into a deep wooded valley beyond, where owls and vultures live. Cool off in the shared kitchen with a selection of good Ventoux wines and homemade snacks. Then chill out for a while in your beautifully designed, spacious room – each one unique, with its own spa bath. For an even more memorable stay, ask about the garden annex or the upstairs 'under the stars' room with a bed on rails that pushes out onto the balcony. Highly recommended.

metafort-provence.com

Le Mas des Oules, Saint-Victor-des-Oules

€€

Le Mas des Oules is a converted farmhouse and stables just 10 minutes' drive from the bustling town of Uzès. It's perfect for families – all of the rooms are self-catering, there's a large swimming pool and plenty of outdoor space, including a peaceful inner courtyard and surrounding lawns and fields for playing games. There are eight rooms in total, each with its own terrace, and all are slightly different in décor – the general vibe is clean and modern. The entire *mas* sleeps 42, and has two large reception rooms if you're looking for somewhere to throw a party or stage an event. If you need to stock up on wine, Domaine Deleuze-Rochetin and Domaine Chabrier are both less than 30 minutes away by car.

lemasdesoules.eu

Metafort

Best fine dining in the Rhône

From hushed, Michelin-starred establishments where you can genuflect at the altar of a great chef, to informal Lyonnais bouchons, lo-fi Natural wine bars and dozens of other choices, the Rhône has so many places to eat, at every level, it's hard to know where to start.

La Pyramide

Pass through the Northern Rhône and there are some fine addresses to keep you going, particularly around Vienne, Tain l'Hermitage and Tournon. Then there's Valence, where Anne-Sophie Pic runs her gleaming culinary empire.

There's no lack of serious restaurants in the Southern Rhône too. Not just around Avignon, but liberally scattered around the map, so no matter where you use as your base, you can always find somewhere nearby to pamper your palate.

Needless to say, we're talking French food here. It's rare to find faithful reproductions of foreign cuisines around these parts. Wine, too, will be local – usually hyper-local. But as criticisms go, these are moot points: you're not on holiday in the Rhône to wash down pizza with Malbec.

Northern Rhône

La Mère Brazier, Lyon

€€€€€

Eugénie Brazier, one of the founding mothers of Lyonnais cuisine, was one of the most lauded chefs of her time. She opened her restaurant in 1921. In 2008, it was bought by chef Mathieu Viannay, and he kept many of the period details and décor, which makes a visit to La Mère Brazier feel like being transported back in time. The food is still classically French, with dishes such as crispy pike mousse with smoked eel and a fresh nettle coulis, and Grand

La Mère Brazier

Where winemakers dine

In Caderousse, just a few minutes from Châteauneuf-du-Pape, **Le Café de France** is a place where you can feel at home. The menu is simple but masterful, sincere and respectful of the seasons and producers. Each plate showcases the local produce with taste and delicacy, in much the same way as a good winegrower works his grapes. This is much more than a restaurant. It's a refuge for epicureans, a haven for enthusiasts, a place where the cuisine speaks the same language as the wine: that of authenticity, terroir and generosity. And then there's the warm, unpretentious welcome. Chef Christophe Bolis is passionate about wine, and his cooking is just like him: generous and authentic. We open bottles here like we share stories: from the heart. Because at Café de France, wine is never just an accompaniment. It's at the centre of the table, the discussion, the moment.

Baptiste Grangeon, Domaine de Cristia, Courthézon (Châteauneuf-du-Pape)

Marnier soufflé with Meyer lemon sorbet and blood orange. Considering the restaurant has two Michelin stars, the wine list is more affordable than you might expect, with plenty of choice under €100 per bottle (and untold gems at the higher end too). Closed at weekends.

lamerebrazier.fr

La Pyramide, Vienne

€€€€€

L'Espace PH3, Vienne

€€€

Having recently celebrated its 200th anniversary, La Pyramide is a gastronomic institution. Now owned by chef Patrick Henriroux, it's held on to two Michelin stars since 1990. Its neighbourhood – suburban Vienne – might not be the most glamorous, but once inside the building, this changes; the dining room of the main restaurant is a stunning space and the food is even more perfect – think green asparagus grilled on a Japanese barbecue, wild garlic coulis, hazelnut tartlet with lemon verbena emulsion. The gastronomic restaurant is just the tip of the iceberg. At the same site, you'll also find the popular bistro L' Espace PH3, where you can eat in the conservatory or garden with a pared-down menu and open chef's station. More

La Pyramide

recently they've opened the Blue Pearl bar where they design their own cocktails and pour from their rare library of Chartreuse – it's open to all, not just diners. They've also opened a collection of rooms and suites (see Best hotels in the Rhône Valley p132). 'The idea is to be always moving, always changing,' says Boris Henriroux, chief executive and son of the chef. So what's next? A nearby wine emporium due to open in 2026 with access to some of the finest, rarest wines in the region – the fourth side of La Pyramide.

lapyramide.com

Les Gagères, Tupin-et-Semons

€€€

Jean-Michel Stéphan, one of the few Natural winemakers in this part of the world, has gained a dedicated following; when his wines are on form, they can be exquisite. Natural wine is often associated with an almost grungy aesthetic – which is what makes the restaurant in his winery, Les Gagères, so surprising. Opening in 2024, the glass-walled dining room has stunning views over the vineyards of Côte-Rôtie. Front of house staff are highly professional, and the cooking

Les Gagères

here is a kind of elevated *bistronomique* style. The wine list has lots of Stéphan's wines – including lots of older vintages, which are hard to find, and priced accordingly. There are lots of other references from other top estates throughout the Northern Rhône and beyond. They've been awarded for their commitment to sustainability, and most of their ingredients are organic. You can expect dishes such as goat's milk panna cotta with chard, green sauce and citron, followed by slow-cooked pork belly with spiced lentils and wild garlic. It's a welcome addition to the Côte-Rôtie dining scene.

lesgageres.fr

Le Cerisier, Tournon

€€€

One of Tournon's most ambitious restaurants, Le Cerisier currently holds a Michelin Bib Gourmand, but it feels like it's aiming for a star. It's split into two rooms, each seating around 15, making for an intimate setting. The service is politely formal, and the sommelier has impressive knowledge of the Northern Rhône – the wine list is long, and you can find plenty of hard-to-find gems at reasonable prices. On the menu, you can expect to start with dishes such as Jerusalem artichoke soup with black truffle, blue cheese panna cotta and caramelized hazelnuts; followed by fillet of pork served with a nose-to-tail croquette and sweet-and-sour sauce.

lecerisier-restaurant.fr

Restaurant Pic, Valence

€€€€€

André, Valence

€€€

Anne-Sophie Pic is one of France's most garlanded chefs and is the third generation of restaurateur in her family. The original family restaurant in Saint-Péray gained three stars in 1934 before they relocated to Valence, and this is still the beating heart of the operation,

with additional sites in Paris, Dubai, Bangkok, London, Paris and beyond. The dining room is decorated in pale grey and powder pink, with a gorgeous eye-height Baccarat chandelier at its centre. Most tables look out into the exotic garden where you can enjoy an aperitif. They have 33,000 bottles of wine in the cellar, 65% Rhône, 25% Burgundy. You name it, they've got it, and it's all been bought direct from the domaine. The bistro André in the same building offers a less elaborate

Restaurant Pic

menu – traditional bistro dishes – and the selection here focuses on Natural and younger winemakers (though you can order from the main list if you ask). They also have very smart rooms and suites if you want to make a weekend of it (see Best hotels in the Rhône Valley p132).

anne-sophie-pic.com

Southern Rhône

La Beaugravière, Mondragon

€€€

If you want to drink the greatest Rhône wines at peak maturity, look no further than the institution that is the Beaugravière. It has an immense cellar, the wines presented on hand-written sheets within an old tome. What makes it particularly thrilling is the amount of very old wines, including back vintages from the most iconic estates of Hermitage, Côte-Rôtie and Châteauneuf-du-Pape. Like the bedrooms, the dining room is plainly decorated and serves its purpose. The location could at best be described as convenient, given its immediate proximity to the A7. But if your priority above all else is great wine – this is where to come. Chef Guy Jullien is still on the pans, having opened the doors in 1976. Other than wine, his other gastronomic obsession is black truffles – during winter months, his menu dedicated to 'black diamonds' is not to be missed.

beaugraviere.com

L'Oustalet, Gigondas

€€€€

Does L'Oustalet in Gigondas have the best Rhône wine list in the world? With 4,000 wines, it's certainly one of them. The depth of choice is extraordinary – a roll-call of the best producers in the region, with plenty of older vintages, hidden gems and rising stars to discover. And the prices, considering it has a Michelin star, are very reasonable. Perhaps this should come as no surprise; the restaurant (along with nearby guest rooms, wine bar and Le Bistrot de l'Oustalet – see Best bistros and wine bars p166) are all owned by the Perrin family of legendary Châteauneuf property Château de Beaucastel. You can sit outside, on the terrasse that borders the airy village square, or inside, in the small but comfortable dining room. You might start with clams, Provence artichoke and sorrel, followed by local pigeon, shallots, radish; then finish with Corsican clementine feuilleté, hazelnut and smoked cream. Eating here is always a memorable occasion.

loustalet-gigondas.fr

La Mère Germaine,

Châteauneuf-du-Pape

€€€€

The Strasser family has played a major role in the elevation of Châteauneuf-du-Pape as a tourist destination. In 2019, they bought the once-great hotel and restaurant La Mère Germaine at the heart of the village and restored both parts of the business to their former glory. The hotel rooms are decorated and equipped to a high standard (see Best hotels in the Rhône Valley p132) and the restaurant gained a Michelin star shortly after opening. The terrace outside has great views, or you can sit in the air-conditioned dining room if the Mistral is blowing. Young head chef Adrien Soro works wonders with the flavours of the south, producing a creative menu of real verve and excitement: parsnip flowers with hazelnut condiment with a meat-like parsnip jus, or Drôme pigeon cooked pink with braised radicchio and crispy Jerusalem artichoke risotto, served with pigeon jus cut with bay leaf oil. The stimulating wine list contains all the Châteauneuf-du-Pape you would hope for, but has plenty of wines from outside the region too, other strengths being Alsace, Loire and Burgundy. The Strassers also own the bistro Le Comptoir de la Mère Germaine, a short walk away.

lameregermaine.com

La Mère Germaine

La Table de Sorgues, Sorgues

€€€

Until Châteauneuf-du-Pape's village makeover in the late 2010s, there was only one good place to eat nearby, and that was La Table de Sorgues. Philippe Cambie, a legendary winemaking consultant and gastronome who worked with many great Châteauneuf estates, was a regular. It might have a bit more competition these days, but it's as good as ever. The owners Stéphane and Stéphanie Riss are originally from Alsace,

La Calade

but after having worked in restaurants around Europe, they settled here, and you can see why they were charmed by the place. The restaurant is located on the ground floor of an old mansion building that dates to 1891 in the village of Sorgues, with a small walled garden and bright dining room. Cooking is classic bistronomique without excess frills, and the wine list focuses on the Rhône. Prices are reasonable.

latabledesorgues.fr

La Calade, Blauvac

€€€

La Calade is a restaurant that is very hard to fault. The food is delicious; intense in flavour, innovative but still Provençal, excellent from amuse bouche to dessert. The wine list has everything you could want from the local area – you could come back every day and not get bored. There are 20 seats inside and 20 outside; both are good options, and share the same magnificent view. Owners Janis and Margaux plan to open a second restaurant in nearby Malemort-du-Comtat in 2026. If it's anything like La Calade, it will be a must-visit.

lacaladeblauvac.fr

La Mirande, Avignon

€€€€€

La Mirande is a flamboyantly beautiful hotel in Avignon (see Best hotels in the Rhône Valley p132) and it's blessed with a number of dining options. The restaurant's Michelin star has recently been joined by a Michelin green star. Chef Florent Pietravalle, who worked for four years as sous-chef in Pierre Gagnaire's three-Michelin-star restaurant in Paris, produces Provençale cuisine that can be enjoyed in the high-ceilinged dining room or the beautiful enclosed garden. Expect dishes such as

La Mirande

sea snail and pork stew with a vegetable sabayon, or celery root with white truffle and chives. An alternative is the lighter touch from the same chef in the bistro La Salle à Manger. Or there's La Table Haute, a shared table downstairs where dishes are cooked in a 19th-century kitchen over a wood-fired range. There's a bar, a tea room and even a pop-up summer tavern. The wine list doesn't disappoint. It's extensive, with plenty from the Southern Rhône, of course, but the Northern Rhône and Burgundy are well represented too.

la-mirande.fr

La Fourchette, Avignon

€€€

Some restaurants manage to feel at once smart and comfortable; La Fourchette, founded in 1960, just behind the main square in Avignon, strikes that balance. The front of house team is unfailingly considerate, and the dishes have been honed over time to really deliver. It's local Provençal cuisine that doesn't try too hard to be inventive, but the quality of the ingredients really shines. You might not come here specifically for the wine list, but you can always find good things to drink.

la-fourchette.eatbu.com

Le Vivier, Isle-sur-la-Sorgue

€€€

The village of Isle-sur-la-Sorgue is exactly that – an island on the river Sorgue, stacked with ancient houses, independent shops and a church at its centre. It has one of the best markets in the region (see Markets p86) and is encircled by a wealth of antiques and interiors shops. There is a dizzying array of cafés and restaurants along the riverbank – it gets very busy at weekends during the summer – many of which serve decent but forgettable fare to hungry tourists. If you're looking for more elevated cooking with a good wine selection, try Le Vivier, just slightly off the main drag. It offers a creative menu that cleverly combines flavours to create memorable dishes, such as foie gras, smoked eel, pear, black cardamom and Earl Grey; finish with mandarin, acacia honey and saffron. Ask to sit on the balcony above the river.

levivier-restaurant.com

La Mère Brazier

Tupin-et-Semons

Best bistros and wine bars

The Rhône is famous for the excellent value of its wines, and for the reasonable mark-ups set by its restaurants and bistros. If there's one grumble, it's the paucity of wines served by the glass. Even bistros that really understand wine, might only serve a handful of reds, whites and rosés, and those will be rarely the most exciting. But perhaps that's not such a big deal, when the wines by the bottle are so affordable. The list that follows is a selection of places where you can eat and drink to a high standard.

Auberge de Crussol

Northern Rhône

Café Terroir, Lyon

€€€

Finding somewhere that can tick all the boxes – food, wine, service and ambiance – is never easy, even in a city like Lyon. Café Terroir manages to pull it off, while still offering a relaxed and informal vibe. It's not a classic Lyon *bouchon*, but rather has a contemporary aesthetic, somewhere between a bistro and a wine bar. You can expect all the Lyonnais classics on the menu – snails, pâte en croute, terrine – plus haut-rôtisserie (if that's a thing), plates of cheese and desserts. The wine list plucks gleaming gems from Burgundy, the Jura and the Rhône. La Cave Café Terroir, the sister wine bar opposite, is also well worth visiting.

cafeterroir.fr

Café Terroir

Café Comptoir Abel

Café Comptoir Abel, Lyon

€€€

The bouchon is a Lyon institution – the name signifies a small, often family-owned, restaurant that serves traditional Lyonnais specialities such as *rosette* (salami), *boudin noir* (black pudding) *saucisson chaud* (sliced hot pork sausage), *tête de veau* (calf's head terrine), *cervelle de canut* (it means 'silk workers' brains' but it's soft cheese and chives) and *andouillette* (tripe sausage). Some bouchons are tourist traps, but others, such as Café Comptoir Abel, are the real deal – it almost looks like a film set, with its wood panelling, ancient posters and restaurant artifacts. The food is hearty and rustic, the service surprisingly friendly, and you can find good things to

Where winemakers dine

Maison Chenet, nestled among vineyards and scrubland in Pujaut, has a history of family and flavours. This unique place, surrounded by vineyards and lavender fields, offers exceptional dishes with the scent of Provence throughout the seasons. This father-and-son team highlights the region's farmers with their authentic gastronomic art. Their work is precise and generous. They are also founding members of the Gard aux Chefs association, whose goal is to promote the traditions of excellence in the Gard region. Chefs, artisans, winemakers... of which Domaine de la Mordorée has been a member since 2022. In a former white stone silkworm farm, **La Courtille** in Tavel is charming and serene, with a beautiful terrace sheltered by a wonderful old cedar tree. Natalia Crozon offers gourmet and regional cuisine. A must-see place where you will be charmed by the finesse and generosity of their cuisine and by the selection of wines.

Ambre Delorme, Domaine de la Mordorée, Tavel

drink on the wine list (go by the bottle). You won't leave hungry. For other reliable bouchons, visit lesbouchonslyonnais.org.

maisonabel.fr

Les Epicurieux, Ampuis

€€

On the one hand, this is a wine shop – a large, square room, its walls crammed with the best of the Northern Rhône. On the other hand, it's a bistro; in the middle of the room are chairs and tables, where you can order the inexpensive set menu with dishes that go well with Côte-Rôtie and Condrieu. Tack a smaller room with posh Burgundy on one side, a slim bar on the other – and you have Les Epicurieux. Owner Arnaud knows the local wine scene inside out – in fact, you're bound to bump into some winemakers on their lunch break.

cavelesepicurieux.fr

Le Bateau Ivre, Tain l'Hermitage

€

If you've had a few blow-out nights in Tain l'Hermitage and you just fancy a plate of cheese or charcuterie, go to Le Bateau Ivre next to the footbridge to Tournon. It's run by a cheerful young team who know what's going on in the local wine scene, but don't worry – it's not all Natural wine, there are all types to choose from. Not to mention local beers – crucial refreshment if you've been tasting wine all day.

+33 (0)7 83 35 06 84

Le Tournesol, Tournon

€€

Le Tournesol gets everything right. The husband-and-wife team are welcoming and friendly. Their wine list is one of the best in town, with very fair prices. And chef Cyril, who naturally understands fine products, creates dishes that you might find yourself ordering multiple times, such is their outrageous deliciousness: truffled croque monsieurs with ham, tartufata and aged gouda; homemade parmesan churros with Majorcan sobrasada mayonnaise; asparagus tartlet with vin jaune foam, morel crumb and morel jus... The table by the door is groaning with digestifs.

letournesol.net

Auberge du Père Monnet, La Roche-de-Glun

€€

A handy stop-off between Tournon and Valence, L'Auberge du Père Monnet is next to the river on a little island in the Rhône called La Roche-de-Glun. It offers simple, no frills, but authentic bistro cooking on a shady terrace. They've recently opened a wine shop next door, and both specialize in Natural wine. Co-owner Eric knows all the local players (not least his winemaker son). This is an invaluable spot to know about if you enjoy low-intervention wines.

+33 (0)4 75 84 57 80

Auberge de Crussol, Saint-Péray

€€€

The pretty village of Saint-Péray is well worth a day trip. When it's time to eat, head up to the Auberge de Crussol. It's a 20-minute hike towards the ruined Château de Crussol, or you can drive up and park in

Auberge de Crussol

their car park. It's the perfect spot to visit no matter the season; in summer, you can sit on the airy terrace and take in the view; in winter, the ancient building has nooks and crannies where you can sit. Ask for a table overlooking the kitchen – they cook local ingredients over a roaring wood fire. Cuts of meat are sold by weight; sausage sold by the metre (vegetarians are less well catered for). The list is short but well chosen, mostly natural-leaning Northern Rhônes.

aubergedecrussol.com

Le Bac à Traille, Valence

€€€

This is the younger sister of the Michelin-starred La Cachette (directly next-door). Le Bac à Traille opened more recently and consists of a small, square dining room that shares the same calm and sober décor as its sibling, just without the large windows. Chef Masashi Ijichi offers a similarly complex and precise cuisine in both restaurants – French with a Japanese accent. The *restaurant gastronomique* next door has an excellent list with over 600 bins;

Le Bac à Traille

Coteaux et Fourchettes

Le Bac usually offers an edited version. You can request the main list however if you want to choose from the full range; it contains many hard-to-find local bottles, along with wines from Italy, Spain and beyond – some natural, some classic.

www.lacachette-valence.fr

Southern Rhône

Coteaux et Fourchettes, Cairanne

€€€

Among the endless vineyards of the Plan de Dieu, Coteaux et Fourchettes is a handy place to know about – it's equidistant from Cairanne, Rasteau and Gigondas, has ample parking and is easy to find. It's right next to a roundabout, but don't let that put you off – it's perfectly tranquil on the terrace behind the restaurant. The style is modern but comfortable and everything here is a cut above: the décor, the service, the ingredients and the wine list. Pair a mature white Cairanne with the comté profiterole stuffed with celery risotto and truffle butter served with green asparagus and a creamy sabayon. Then enjoy a young Gigondas with half a roast pigeon with confit leg, variation of carrots, turnips glazed with orange and argan oil with a cumin jus. Finish the meal with a sweet Rasteau.

coteauxetfourchettes.com

Le Bistrot de l'Oustalet and Le Nez, Gigondas

€€€

The Michelin-starred L'Oustalet (see Best fine dining in the Rhône p152) is one of three bars and restaurants in Gigondas owned by the Perrin family of Château de Beaucastel. The other two – the Bistrot de l'Oustalet and wine bar Le Nez – also excel at their respective levels. The cooking at the Bistrot is heartier than its sibling, offering vibrant flavours and dishes that really satisfy, such as rack of Ventoux pork with confit aubergine and grilled courgettes; or a rib of beef smoked with thyme with goats cheese potato gratin and a green salad. Ask to sit in the garden. Le Nez next door occupies a little square where you can stop for a glass and some snacks if you're just passing through. Both places benefit from warm and knowledgeable staff, and all three establishments share the same cellar, so you can drink extraordinarily well whichever one you visit.

loustalet-gigondas.fr

Vin Ensen, Caromb

€€

If wine is your priority, go to Vin Ensen. This bar restaurant at the heart of the village of

Vin Ensen

Caromb appears pleasant if unremarkable, but open the wine list and you'll see why this place is so special – it's a thrilling line-up of Burgundy, Provence, Jura… but mostly Rhône, including lots of hard-to-find producers, for very reasonable prices. Unusually for the Rhône, there is even an exciting list of wines by the glass – and if you don't see anything that takes your fancy, they'll open something specially. You can sit inside or out the front for lunch, and they open their rear terrace (with its great views) for dinner. What's more, they've just opened a boutique opposite to sell bottles to take away.

vinensen.com

Café de France, Caderousse

€€€

The sleepy village of Caderousse (population about 2,600) is a 15-minute drive northwest of Châteauneuf-du-Pape. It's home to several ancient churches, a couple of small châteaux, and the restaurant of Corsican chef Christophe Bolis, Café de France. He is one of those chefs who instinctively understands food – particularly meat – and he loves to feed people. It's impossible not to eat well here; how about green asparagus with burnt lemon and smoked egg yolk vinaigrette? Or lobster ravioli with Thai basil? The wine

list is huge, packed with gems, and very reasonably priced.

cafe-defrance.fr

Le Verger des Papes, Châteauneuf-du-Pape

€€€

If you saunter up through the village of Châteauneuf-du-Pape to look at the ruined château (which you must), you'll walk past Le Verger des Papes near the top of the hill. It's a good place to stop for lunch. It has a shady, landscaped terrace where you can take in the amazing views, but if you don't like the summer heat ask for an indoor table. The hearty Provençal cooking is a good match for robust wines, and naturally there is an extensive list of red and white Châteauneuf to choose from.

vergerdespapes.com

Chez Serge, Carpentras

€€€

Do you like truffles? Then pay a visit to Carpentras institution Chez Serge. Monsieur Ghoukassian knows them better than anyone, and during truffle season this is the place to go. The restaurant is a warren of cosy little rooms around a small central courtyard. The wine list deserves to win all the

Le Verger des Papes

awards – naturally the Southern Rhône is well represented, but you can find good Northern Rhône, Champagne, Burgundy, Bordeaux and Languedoc. If it's full (it's wise to book in advance) then you can try their wine bar just over the road, Le Petit Serge, which is open Thursday to Sunday. They also sell bottles to take away.

chez-serge.fr

La Fille des Vignes, Uzès

€€

Looking for an inexpensive place to eat in Uzès with a decent choice of wines? Try La Fille des Vignes in the little Place Albert 1er. It's somewhere between a café and a restaurant – you can drop in for coffee, breakfast, lunch, dinner or just a cool beer to watch the world go by. The main menu has classic French bistro fare: steak frites, hamburger, Caeser salad, cheese plates... all made with good-quality local ingredients. Plentiful pastries and desserts make it a hit with kids too.

restaurantlafilledesvignes.fr

Le 46, Avignon

€€

You can use Le 46 however you like – it's open all day for drinks and snacks, or you can come from a full lunch or dinner. They

Where winemakers dine

One of my personal favourites, **Le Moulin** in Lourmarin should not be missed. The menu changes regularly, depending on the harvest and the daily catch, offering a mix of traditional Provençal dishes with a creative twist, as well as fresh produce from the grill. The plates are designed to be shared, creating a warm and sociable dining experience, exactly what I look for when I go out for lunch or dinner. The restaurant combines fine dining with a relaxed atmosphere, set in a beautiful environment. The wine list follows the same philosophy, offering high-quality, unpretentious wines that perfectly complement the meal.

Valentine Tardieu-Vitali, Château la Verrerie, Puget (Luberon)

source a lot of products such as cheese and charcuterie from Les Halles, the Avignon temple of fresh ingredients. There's even a little wine shop corner, which is handy, as they really know their wine here – the list has over 500 bottles, mostly but not exclusively from the Southern Rhône. The vibe is informal, the team is welcoming, and there's even a friendly golden retriever. Great chips too.

le46avignon.com

La Cabane d'Oléron, Avignon

€

It doesn't look much: the 'cabin' is essentially a lean-to tacked on to the rear of Les Halles. But don't be put off – it's busy for a reason. The seafood here is the best in town: metal platters of incredibly fresh oysters, prawns and whelks stacked on towers whisked to your table along with little tubs of aioli. The wine isn't the best you'll find, but sometimes – just sometimes – a tumbler of cheap Picpoul de Pinet is all you need.

+33 (0)6 98 29 10 88

Restaurant l'Agape, Avignon

€€€

Some restaurant-lined squares in France are tourist traps. The Place des Corps Saints in the southern part of Avignon, however, is quite the opposite. During weekend lunchtimes and evenings it bustles with busy waiters, tinkling glasses and young children playing in the disused fountain – all overlooked by a 14th century church. Restaurant l'Agape has a sizeable space both inside and

Restaurant l'Agape

on the square itself, serving dishes such as green asparagus soup, asparagus tartare, with fresh herb-whipped cream with shallots; and roasted trout with almonds, spelt risotto and langoustine bisque. All very wine-friendly – which is ideal, as they have the best wine list on the *place*.

restaurant-agape-avignon.com

L'Insolite, Lourmarin

€€

On the long list of villages to visit in the Luberon, Lourmarin is among the loveliest. It's big and varied enough to spend a day wandering the streets here, visiting the bohemian independent shops, the castle – and the plentiful places to eat and drink. A reliable, informal, (relatively) inexpensive spot is L'Insolite – classic Provençal cuisine, friendly service and a calm but vibrant atmosphere. Friday is market day in Lourmarin, so it's a good a good day to visit – but make sure you book well in advance.

brasserie-linsolite.fr

Atelier des Halles, Saint Gilles

€€€

If you're spending some time exploring Costières de Nîmes and the Camargue, then Nîmes itself is an obvious place to stop for lunch or dinner. If you're looking for somewhere off the beaten track, consider Saint Gilles. It has a certain faded charm, and you can stop at the Atelier des Halles for lunch. You can opt for sharing boards, salads or a full menu – start with some Camargue oysters, follow with cod loin with young vegetables and a herbed brandade purée, then finish with a home-made raspberry and white chocolate tartlet. The wine list is short, features many of the best names in Costières de Nîmes, and offers great value for money. After lunch, go and take a look around the 12th-century church known as the Abbatiale Saint-Gilles – the façade alone is worth the visit.

www.atelierdeshalles.fr

Atelier des Halles

Best wine shops

You're in the Rhône Valley, surrounded by wineries, so you might think a visit to a wine shop would be unnecessary. But there are many good reasons to browse the shelves of a good caviste. Some estates don't accept visitors, or might be closed when you want to call. At a wine shop you can buy mixed cases of bottles from different producers, and wine shop staff can be great sources of independent information about the region, under-the-radar villages, up-and-coming producers, local restaurants... And what if you need a bottle of Champagne?

Le Caveau du Gigondas

Northern Rhône

Antic Wine, Lyon

Last time I was there, the staff member at Antic Wine in Lyon who served me dropped a free homemade saucisson in my shopping bag. This is just one reason I'll be going back to Antic Wine. It's a small, chaotic wine shop where you can find some extremely good bottles from the Rhône and Burgundy, including lots of magnums and hard-to-find treats. Owner Georges dos Santos is energetic, opinionated and obsessed with wine, and his shop in the old town embodies everything that is good about small, independent wine merchants.

+33 (0)4 78 37 08 96

Vinothèque de Serine, Ampuis

There are a couple of good options for buying wine in Ampuis. Next door to Le Bistrot de Serine (see Best bistros and wine bars p166) is their wine shop, Vinothèque de Serine. If there's anything on their wine list that takes your fancy – but you don't have the capacity to drink there and then – you can fill your car boot after lunch. A cunning trick on their part that I happily fall for every time I visit. Expect a huge range of Côte-Rôtie, Condrieu and Saint-Joseph, but all Northern Rhône

Where winemakers dine

Our region boasts extraordinary dining experiences really worth celebrating. At **Chez Alexandre** (two Michelin stars) in Garons, Michel Kayser elevates Mediterranean ingredients with masterful technique and creativity. Thanks to his wife Monique, warmth and elegance reign, while sommelier Lionel Delsol's intuitive pairings enhance every dish. The intimate **Ousta Maï** in Saint-Maximin offers a different charm. Jean-Paul Lecroq works his culinary magic in an open kitchen, crafting memorable dishes, while his wife Sandrine, with her remarkable talent for discovering wines, curates a selection that delights. To wind down, our pick is **Entre 2 Tapas** in Nîmes, where tables are joined as strangers share conversation, great food and intriguing wines. Thanks to Yohan and his team, it's buzzing, generous and full of flavour.

Michel Gassier, Château de Nages, Caissargues (Costières de Nîmes)

appellations are available. The other good place in Ampuis to buy wine to take away is Les Epicurieux, five minutes' walk up the road.

bistrotdeserine.net/vinotheque

La Bouteillerie, Condrieu

If you're travelling through Condrieu on the main D386, you'll pass La Bouteillerie. Naturally, they have an extensive range of Côte-Rôtie and Condrieu, but you can also find some excellent wines from the Southern Rhône and further afield. The range is well chosen, starting with inexpensive IGP wines, all the way up to mature vintages of Guigal's single-vineyard Côte-Rôties.

labouteillerie.com

La Compagnie de l'Hermitage, Tain l'Hermitage

In Tain l'Hermitage, there are two wine shops, both owned by Georges Lelektsoglou, or Georges Le Grec as he's affectionately known. He's been trading wine from the village for decades and is known by all the local winemakers. It's worth taking a look in both shops, but many of the top bottles are held at the Avenue Dr Paul Durand branch. If you're lucky, Georges might show you a few of his real unicorn bottles… but you'll need very deep pockets to walk away with them.

hermite.fr

Cave aux Cinq Sens, Tain l'Hermitage

As you approach La Cave aux Cinq Sens, you'd be forgiven for feeling apprehensive. After all, this isn't some antique, subterranean cellar – it's a modern unit on a commercial estate next to a supermarket near the motorway. So if you're looking for romance and Instagrammable dusty bottles, this isn't for you; if you're looking for an exceedingly good range of Northern Rhône wines at reasonable prices, step right in. If you're interested in spirits and local beers, they can help there too – the team is young and knowledgeable. They also have branches in Vienne, Valence and Salaise-sur-Sanne (between Côte-Rôtie and Hermitage).

caveauxcinqsens.com

Southern Rhône

Maison Moga, Isle-sur-la-Sorgue

If you're visiting Isle-sur-la-Sorgue, make sure you pop into Maison Moga. It's essentially a high-end delicatessen that specializes in cheese, charcuterie

Maison Moga

and wine (but you can find lots of other delicious edibles). It's not a big store, but they pack a lot in – you can buy to take away, or you can order platters of meat or cheese to eat on their covered terrace with a glass of rosé. The wine corner may not be huge, but it is exceptionally well chosen, with great picks all the way from picnic wines up to hard-to-find and rare bottles. Rhône and Provence are the stars, of course, but their range of Champagne is also pretty smart.

maisonmoga.fr

Le Caveau du Gigondas, Gigondas

In some wine villages, the main square is best avoided – too many big-volume brands and tourist traps. That's not the case in Gigondas, where the boutiques are owned by leading producers such as Moulin de la Gardette and Domaine du Terme. You'll also find Le Caveau du Gigondas, which is something a bit different. Organized by the Gigondas wine producers association, you can buy over 100 different Gigondas wines here – all for sale at the same price as you would find them direct from the estate. You can buy by the bottle or the case, and – best of all – you can taste them before you buy.

gigondas-vin.com/boutique

Vinadéa, Châteauneuf-du-Pape

There are numerous little boutiques and cellars dotted around Châteauneuf-du-Pape. What makes Vinadéa different is that the shop is owned by the association of local winemakers. This is good news for several reasons. First, you can choose from a huge number of local estates (many other local boutiques are owned by individual estates). Second, the prices in the shop are the same as you would pay at the estate itself – so prices are low, and you can buy by the bottle or the case. Third, the staff have great knowledge of not just the different estates, but of the appellation and its terroir more widely. To top it off, they can usually organize international shipping.

www.vinadea.com

Le Pot du Vin, Uzès

Who doesn't love a shop with a verdant open-air courtyard? Les Pots d'Uzès has one, where you can mill around choosing which large terracotta vessels would look best on the terrasse of your imaginary villa. Keep going towards the back and you'll find some stairs that lead you down deep into the cool, damp basement of Le Pot du Vin, the perfect atmosphere for storing wine. Lots of gems to uncover here, including some slightly older bottles, which aren't always easy to find – mostly Rhône, Provence and Languedoc.

+33 (0)6 03 22 68 97

Cave de Chaz, Villeneuve-lès-Avignon

Robin Chazalon opened his shop just a few years ago in Villeneuve-lès-Avignon. I'm not sure how he's managed to accrue so much knowledge so young (in part it's because his father's a winemaker), but it's stacked with some of the most exciting names in Rhône wines – and plenty of options from other French regions, including the Loire, Burgundy, Languedoc, Corsica... It's a good place to winkle out some of the Rhône's rarer bottles and he even has some serious bottles from outside France – sacré bleu!

cavedechaz.com

Cave de Chaz

Liquid

Liquid, Avignon

Conveniently placed just a minute's walk from Les Halles in Avignon, Cave Liquid is a winning combination of impressive range and excellent service. Hugues Imperiali (pictured with his son Oscar) opened the store in 2003, and his easy-going demeanour belies his impressive depth of knowledge of Rhône and Provençal wines. If you're looking for a gift for a wine lover, he also stocks a massive range of wine accessories. International shipping can usually be arranged.

woowine.com/cavistes/avignon-liquid

Where winemakers dine

Comptoir 1940 is a 35-seat restaurant named after the year that Condrieu became an appellation. It evokes a chic, post-war French bistro where winegrowers happily rub shoulders with villagers and wine-loving tourists – all welcomed by owner Laëtitia's unwavering smile. The wine list naturally features Northern Rhône wines; Burgundy and Champagne are also noteworthy. The co-owner and sommelier Thomas acquired a solid restaurant background before setting out with Laëtitia; the cuisine is classically French with a modern touch in the presentation of the dishes. The cheese offering is 100% local. Highly recommended.

Xavier Gérard, Domaine Xavier Gérard, Condrieu

Auberge de Crussol

Glossary

acidity an essential component of wine, providing freshness and balance

amphore an amphora, a large clay vessel used to age and ferment wines

argile clay, a common soil type in the Southern Rhône

assemblage blend of grape varieties

barrique a small wooden barrel, usually made of oak, with a typical volume of either 225 litres or 228 litres (usually the latter in the Rhône)

béton concrete; concrete tanks are used for fermentation and maturing wines, particularly reds, and can give excellent results

bois literally 'wood'; usually refers to barrels

calcaire limestone, a common soil type in the Southern Rhône

cave the cellar, where the grapes are transformed into wine

cépage grape variety

chai barrel room

chaillées terraces on slopes built to support vines in the Northern Rhône

chêne literally 'oak'; usually refers to barrels

cuve a large tank used to ferment and age wines, usually made of concrete or oak

cuvée a term with multiple meanings, usually used to refer to a specific wine in a producer's range (literally means 'blend')

demi-muid medium-sized wooden barrel, usually made of oak, with a typical volume of 600 litres

échalas tall wooden stakes used to support single grapevines, commonly used in the Northern Rhône for Syrah

élevage literally the 'raising' or 'upbringing' of the wine, in other words the maturation or ageing of the wine, usually in wooden barrels

foudre generic term for a large wooden barrel, usually made of oak, that can vary in size between 10 and 120 hectolitres

galets roulés large rounded river pebbles, a common rock type in the Southern Rhône

garrigue scrubland; wines of the Southern Rhône are sometimes said to evoke the wild herbs that grow there

gneiss a common rock type in the Northern Rhône

gobelets vines not supported on wires, sometimes called 'bush vines' in English

granit granite, a common rock type in the Northern Rhône

inox stainless steel; stainless steel tanks are used for fermenting and maturing wines, particularly white wines

loess wind-blown sand, a common soil type in the Southern and Northern Rhône

mistral cold, drying north wind; can be violent

rafle grape stems

sable sand, a common soil type in the Southern Rhône

safre a Provençal term referring to a hard sandstone that turns into sand after weathering

schist a common rock type in the Northern Rhône

sélection parcellaire a wine made from the fruit of a single special vineyard

structure the elements of the wine that you can feel in the mouth (salinity, acidity, tannin, bitterness, etc.) rather than its flavours

tannin a natural compound in wine, derived from grape skins, seeds and oak, that contributes to its texture, structure and ageing potential

terroir the unique combination of permanent or semi-permanent natural features where vines are grown such as soil, climate and topography that influence the style of the wine

vendange entière the whole grape cluster, both grapes and stems

vieilles vignes literally 'old vines'; no legal definition, but usually refers to vines of at least 50 years of age

vin nature Natural wine; a wine made organically or biodynamically with no other additives (apart from occasionally some sulphur dioxide), made with the least manipulation possible

vinification the process of converting grapes into wine, including fermentation and ageing

Further reading

Wine

Drinking with the Valkyries: Writings on Wine, Andrew Jefford, Académie du Vin Library 2022

There is no greater drinks writer in the English language. If any book can make you fall in love with wine, it's this one.

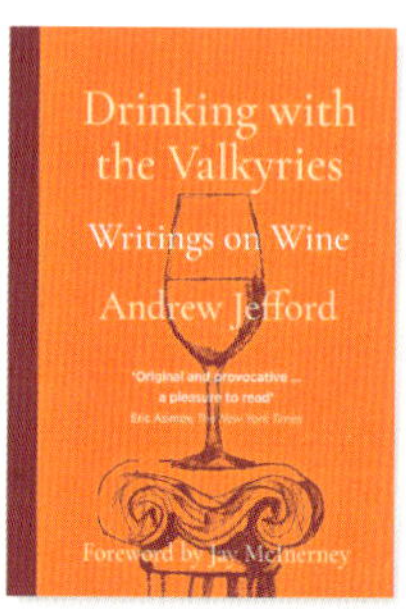

Overviews

The World Atlas of Wine, Hugh Johnson and Jancis Robinson, Mitchell Beazley 2019

Indispensable for everyone with an interest in wine, and helpfully positions the Rhône in a global context.

Wines of the Rhône, Matt Walls, Infinite Ideas 2021

When I was studying wine, there was no book on the Rhône that covered all the appellations, grapes and leading estates all in one place. I wrote this to fill that gap.

The Wines of the Rhône, John Livingstone-Learmonth, Faber & Faber 1992 (3rd edition)

Few authors have been writing about the wines of the Rhône for as long as John, who has been visiting the region since 1973.

Wines of the Rhône Valley, Robert M. Parker Jr, Simon & Schuster 1997

Robert Parker, the most consequential American wine journalist, has a love for the wines of the Rhône that's evident in this tome.

Specific appellations and related regions

The Châteauneuf-du-Pape Wine Book, Harry Karis, Kavino 2009

Everything you need to know about this huge and storied appellation.

Gigondas: Its wines, its land, its people, John Livingstone-Learmonth, Les Editions du Bottin Gourmand 2012

An ode to this jewel of a village, its winemakers and its wines.

Tavel: The people and the wines, Rolf Bischel, Féret 2011

An intriguing look at this unique Rhône rosé.

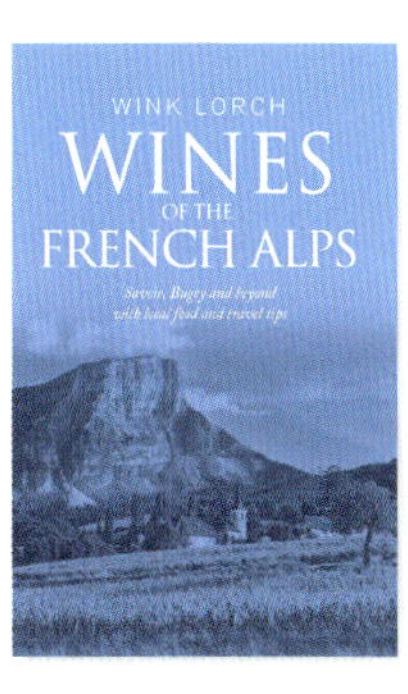

Wines of the French Alps, Wink Lorch, Wine Travel Media 2019

If you're looking for information on the wines of the Diois, Jura or Savoie, let Wink be your guide.

American Rhône: How Maverick Winemakers Changed the Way Americans Drink, Patrick J. Comiskey, University of California Press 2016

How a charismatic bunch of hardscrabble US winemakers embraced Rhône varieties and created some beautiful expressions all of their own.

Grapes and soils

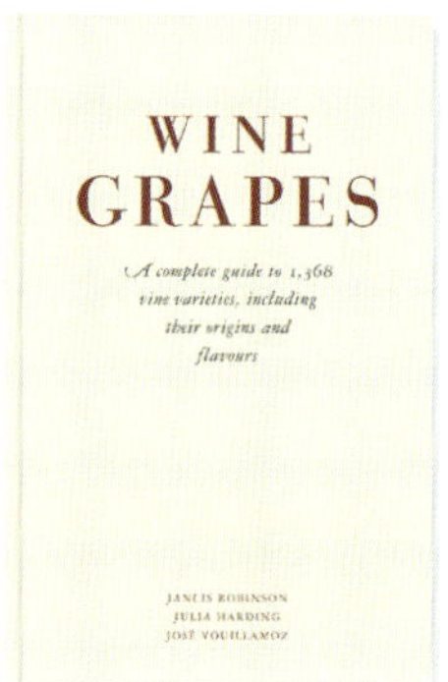

Wine Grapes, Jancis Robinson, Julia Harding, José Vouillamoz, Allen Lane 2012

A beautifully produced guide to the 1,368 vine varieties producing commercially available wine from around the world.

Syrah, Grenache & Mourvèdre, Giles MacDonogh, Penguin 1992

A concise guide to the triumvirate of Southern Rhône red grapes.

Phylloxera, Christy Campbell, HarperCollins 2004

A rollicking read that investigates the rapacious bug that nearly wiped out the vineyards of France in the late 19th century.

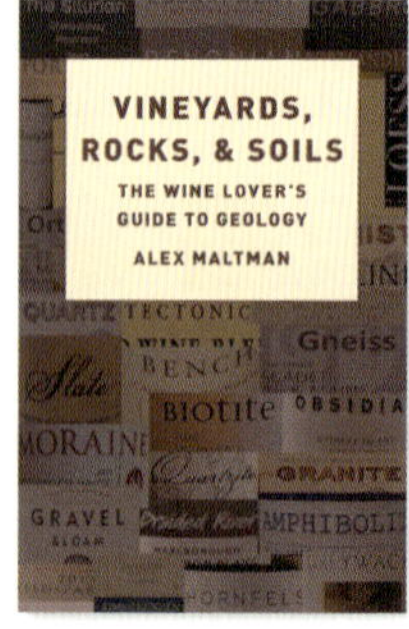

Vineyards, Rocks, & Soils: The Wine Lover's Guide to Geology, Alex Maltman, Oxford University Press 2018

An essential companion for wine lovers seeking to understand rocks and soil, and their influence on their favourite bottles.

Châteauneuf-du-Pape

Index

Acknowledgements

The publishers have made every effort to trace the copyright holders of the text and images reproduced in this book. If, however, you believe that any work has been incorrectly credited or used without permission, please contact us immediately and we will endeavour to rectify the situation.

1 shutterstock.com/ barmalini, 4bl, 25 shutterstock.com/ Kojin, 4br, 66 shutterstock.com/ PRILL, 5bl, 87 shutterstock.com/ trabantos, 5br, La Mère Brazier, Lyon, 8 E.Guigal S.A.S. Chateau d'Ampuis, 12-13 Clara Rieux - Chapelle Saint-Christophe Hermitage, Tain l'Hermitage et Tournon, 14 Palais des Papes, ENoveJosserand / Avignon Tourisme, 15 Massilia, Greek Colony, Pierre Puvis de Chavannes, 1868-1869, 16 Portrait of Pope John XXII Dueze, Giuseppe Franchi, Pinacoteca Ambrosiana, Milan, 18 Baron Pierre Le Roy de Boiseaumarié, Wikipedia Commons, 20 courtesy of Rhône Valley Vineyards, 21 courtesy of Rhône Valley Vineyards, 22 shutterstock.com/ Richard Semik, 23 shutterstock.com/ BearFotos, 28 shutterstock.com/ saiko3p, 30 shutterstock/.com/ Sandra Alkado, 31 © Instapades Studio, 32 shutterstock.com/ Richard Semik, 34 Inter Rhône, Avignon, 36t Inter Rhône, Avignon, 36b Inter Rhône, Avignon, 37t Inter Rhône, Avignon, 37b shutterstock.com/ Sylvie Lebchek, 38 Inter Rhône, Avignon, 39t Inter Rhône, Avignon, 39b Inter Rhône, Avignon, 40t Inter Rhône, Avignon, 40b shutterstock.com/ barmalini, 41t Inter Rhône, Avignon, 41b Inter Rhône, Avignon, 42t shutterstock.com/ Torruzzlo, 42b Inter Rhône, Avignon, 43b Inter Rhône, Avignon, 44 © VPA – Alain Hocquel, 45 © VPA – Alain Hocquel, 46-47 E.Guigal S.A.S. Chateau d'Ampuis, 48 © VPA – Alain Hocquel, 49 © VPA – Alain Hocquel, 50 © VPA – Alain Hocquel, 51 shutterstock.com/ Souchon Yves, 52 Domaine de Beaurenard - Paul Coulon & Fils, 60 courtesy of Châteauneuf -du-Pape, 61 courtesy of Châteauneuf -du-Pape, 62 shutterstock.com/ Alexey Fedorenko, 64 shutterstock.com/ Florine Lambert, 66b shutterstock.com/ michusa, 67 shutterstock.com/ sebchalaye, 70 shutterstock.com/ Pernelle Voyage, 72 shutterstock.com/ ALTV, 73 shutterstock.com/ Pi-R photos, 74 © VPA – Alain Hocquel, 75cr shutterstock.com/ bonchan, 75b shutterstock.com/ page frederique, 76 shutterstock.com/ Watson Creation, 78 © VPA – Alain Hocquel, 79 shutterstock.com/ Saad315, 80-81 Domaine de Saint-Préfert, Famille Isabel Ferrando, 82 Domaine Peylong & L'angle de vue - Lionel Pascale, Juan Robert, Fabien Lombard, 85 Creative Commons 4.0, 86 shutterstock.com/ 1046050312, 87t shutterstock.com/ DeymosHR, 88 shutterstock.com/ Joao Paulo V Tinoco, 89t shutterstock.com/ Fotokon, 89b shutterstock.com/ Ihor Serdyukov, 90t shutterstock.com/ EnJoyce Fotografie, 90b shutterstock.com/ Richard Semik, 91cr shutterstock.com/ MARTIN Florent, 91b shutterstock.com/ Bruno M Photographie, 92t shutterstock.com/ ventdusud, 92c shutterstock.com/ Serge Goujon, 92b shutterstock.com/ page frederique, 93t shutterstock.com/ Mike Workman, 93c shutterstock.com/ DaLiu, 93b shutterstock.com/ BOULENGER Xavier, 94 Tupins et Semons © Instapades Studio, 95 shutterstock.com/ Dietwal, 97cr shutterstock.com/ Michel PERES, 97br shutterstock.com/ Daniel Gauthier, 98-99 shutterstock.com/ jorrisg, 100 shutterstock.com/ jlf06, 101 shutterstock.com/ Marcello Brunetti, 103cr shutterstock.com/ ecstk22, 103b shutterstock.com/ Alexey Fedorenko, 104 shutterstock.com/ Tanja Midgardson, 105t shutterstock.com/ steve estvanik, 105c shutterstock.com/ Erwin Bosman, 105b shutterstock.com/ page frederique, 106t shutterstock.com/ L.Danis, 106b shutterstock.com/ Majonit, 107 shutterstock.com/ Rolf E. Staerk, 108 shutterstock.com/ Pi-R photos, 109 shutterstock.com/ Georgios Tsichlis, 111 shutterstock.com/ RVillalon, 112 shutterstrock.com/ Photoprofi30, 113 shutterstock.com/ FineBokeh, 114-115 © VPA – Alain Hocquel, 117 Domaine de Beaurenard - Paul Coulon & Fils, 118 E.Guigal S.A.S. Chateau d'Ampuis, 119 Michel Chapoutier, Maison M. Chapoutier, Tain l'Hermitage, 120 Domaine M. Chapoutier, Tain l'Hermitage, 121 Maison Delas Frères, Tain L'Hermitage, 123 Domaine Peylong & L'angle de vue - Lionel Pascale, Juan Robert, Fabien Lombard, 124 Domaine des Escaravailles, Rasteau, 125 Jacques Grange, Maison Delas Frères, Tain L'Hermitage, 127 Domaine le Sang des Cailloux, Sarrians, 128 Domaine de Beaurenard - Paul Coulon & Fils, 129 Domaine de la Mordorée, Tavel, 130 Château La Verrerie, Luberon , 131 Château de Nages, Caissargues, 132 InterContinental® Lyon – Hotel Dieu, 134 InterContinental® Lyon – Hotel Dieu, 135 Fabien Lombard, Domaine Peylong & L'angle de vue - Lionel Pascale, Juan Robert, Fabien Lombard, 136 Fac&Spera Hotel&SPA, 137 Pic Hôtel, Relais & Châteaux, 138 Villa Sainte Anne, Île-de-Porquerolles , 139 Hôtel restaurant La Mère Germaine, Châteauneuf-du-Pape, 140 Madeline Ferran, Domaine des Escaravailles, Rasteau, 141 La Mirande, Avignon, 142 Cabanes Perchées, Wow Safari Peaugres, 144 Le Clos de la Garelle, Hotel de la Villeon, Tournon-sur-Rhône, 145 La Tour du Pavillon, Maison M. Chapoutier, Tain L'Hermitage, 146 La Péniche Bed and Bicycle, Tournon, 147 Cabanes Perchées, Wow Safari Peaugres, 148 Frédéric Chaudière,Château Pesquié, Mormoiron (Ventoux), 149 La Verrière, Crestet, 150 Domaine de Saint-Préfert, Famille Isabel Ferrando, 151 Metafort, Méthamis, 152 Hôtel La Pyramide, Vienne, Jonathan Thevenet, 153 La Mère Brazier, Lyon, 154 Baptiste Grangeon, Domaine de Cristia, Courthézon (Châteauneuf-du-Pape), 155 Restaurant Espace Ph3 à l'Hôtel La Pyramide, Vienne, Jonathan Thevenet, 156 Les Gagères, Tupin-et-Semons, 157a Le Cerisier, Tournon, 157b Anne-Sophie Pic à Pic Hôtel, Relais & Châteaux, 159 La Mère Germaine, Châteauneuf-du-Pape, 160 La Calade Hotel Restaurant, Blauvac, 161 La Mirande Restaurant à l'Hôtel La Mirande, Avignon , 163 La Mère Brazier, Lyon, 164-165 Les Gagères, Tupin-et-Semons, 166 Auberge de Crussol, Saint-Péray, 167a Café Terroir, Lyon, 167b Café Comptoir Abel, Lyon, 168 Ambre Delorme, Domaine de la Mordorée, Tavel, 169 Auberge de Crussol, Saint-Péray, 170 Le Bac à Traille, Valence, 171 Côteaux & Fourchettes, Cairanne, 172-173 Vin Ensen, Caromb, 174 Les Verger des Papes, Châteauneuf-du-Pape, 175 Valentine Tardieu-Vitali,Château la Verrerie, Puget (Luberon), 176 Restaurant l'Agape, Avignon, 177 Atelier des Halles, Saint-Gilles, 178 Le Caveau du Gigondas, Gigondas, 179 Michel Gassier, Château de Nages, Caissargues (Costières de Nîmes), 181 Maison Moga, Isle-sur-la-Sorgue, 182 Cave de Chaz, Villeneuve-lès-Avignon, 183t Cave Liquid, Avignon, 183b Xavier Gérard, Domaine Xavier Gérard, Condrieu, 184-185 Auberge de Crussol, Saint-Péray, 191 shuttersatock.com/ Richard Semik

Also available in

The Smart Traveller's Wine Guide series

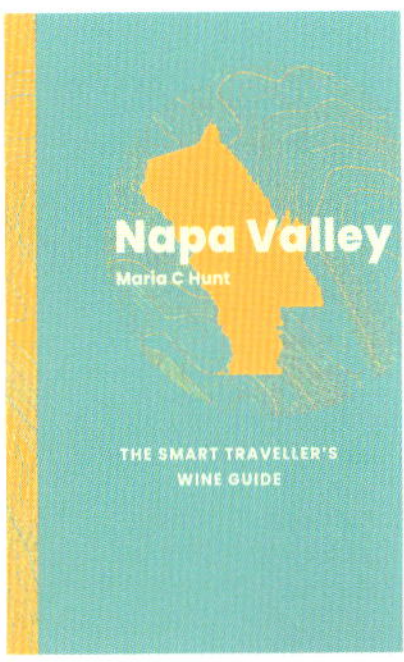

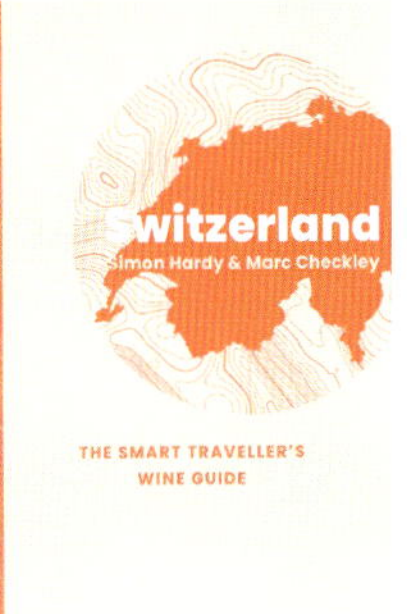

www.academieduvinlibrary.com

Other books from Académie du Vin Library we think you'll enjoy

The Cynic's
Guide to
Wine

Sunny Hodge

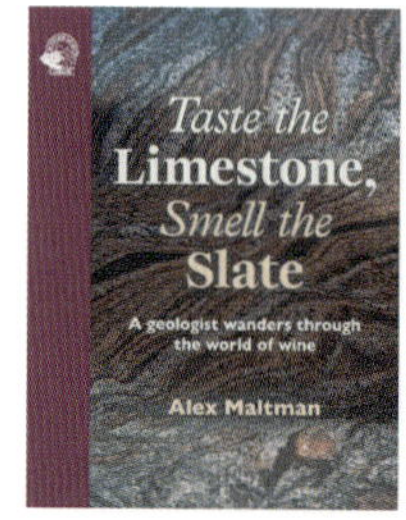

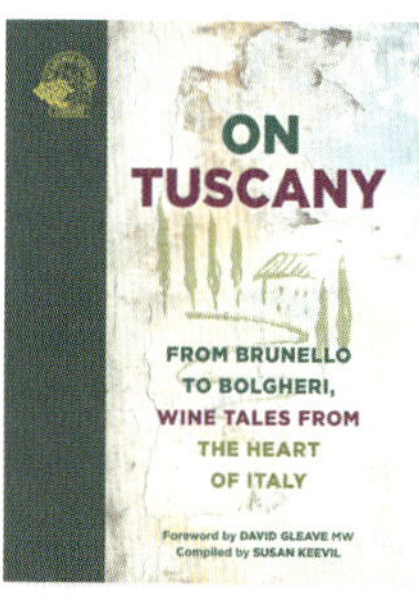

www.academieduvinlibrary.com

HOSPITALITY IN A BOTTLE

RHÔNE VALLEY
VINEYARDS

WWW.VINS-RHONE-TOURISME.FR